basic
Live Sound

D0717011

Published by **SMT**®
an imprint of Bobcat Books Limited
14-15 Berners Street, London W1T 3LJ, UK

Exclusive Distributors:
Music Sales Limited
Distribution Centre, Newmarket Road,
Bury St Edmunds, Suffolk IP33 3YB, UK
Music Sales Corporation
7 Park Avenue South, New York, NY10010
United States Of America
Music Sales Pty Limited
120 Rothschild Avenue,
Rosebery, NSW 2018, Australia

Order No. SMT1914R
ISBN 1-86074-271-8
© Copyright 2003 Paul White
published under exclusive licence by SMT, an imprint and registered trade mark of
Bobcat Books Limited, part of The Music Sales Group.

The Author hereby asserts his/her right to be identified as the author of this work in accordance
with Sections 77 to 78 of the Copyright, Designs and Patents Act 1988.

All rights reserved. No part of this book may be reproduced in any form or by any electronic or
mechanical means, including information storage or retrieval systems, without permission in
writing from the publisher, except by a reviewer who may quote brief passages.
Every effort has been made to trace the copyright holders of the photographs in this book but one
or two were unreachable. We would be grateful if the photographers concerned would contact us.

Printed in the EU

A catalogue record for this book is available from the British Library.

www.musicsales.com

basic
Live Sound

WITHDRAWN

Rotherham College of Arts and Technology

R75743

Paul White

Also by Paul White and available from SMT:

Creative Recording 1 – Effects And Processors (second edition)
*Creative Recording 2 – Microphones, Acoustics, Soundproofing
    And Monitoring* (second edition)
Home Recording Made Easy (second edition)
EMERGENCY! First Aid For Home Recording
MIDI For The Technophobe (second edition)
Recording And Production Techniques

Also by Paul White in this series:

basic Digital Recording
basic Effects And Processors
basic Home Studio Design
basic Mastering
basic Microphones
basic MIDI
basic Mixers
basic Mixing Techniques
basic Multitracking
basic Sampling
basic VST Effects
basic VST Instruments

THE LEARNING CENTRES
ACC No. RM5M43
DATE 27.9.12
CLASS 621.389 WHI

CONTENTS

INTRODUCTION

This book is a down-to-earth, practical guide to choosing and using PA equipment and backline amplification in the context of small to medium-sized gigs. Even relatively inexpensive equipment can produce exceptionally good results when used properly, so if you've ever wondered how to set up your PA so that it doesn't feed back, or how to mic up a drum kit, then this book is written with you in mind.

All elements of live sound are investigated, from choosing the right mic for the job to setting up your PA, back line, effects and monitor system. Subjects covered also include tuning, miking instruments, DI techniques, radio mics, basic wiring and even performance tips.

1 THE PA SYSTEM

Although we tend to take PA systems for granted, technology has actually advanced quite a lot since the early days of sound systems. Big systems have become even bigger, but new technology also allows portable systems to be made smaller, lighter and more powerful, which is good news for performing bands.

In the context of live music, PA – or sound reinforcement, as it is sometimes called – might best be described as a system that helps increase the volume of existing backline instruments and vocals or, in larger venues, provides the bulk of the front-of-house sound. For larger venues or tours it's usual to hire a PA system and a mix engineer, but for pubs, clubs, smaller college venues and so on it's common for bands to have their own systems. A modern stereo PA system capable of delivering several hundreds of watts of power can be small enough to fit into a hatchback car or a small van. It's important, however, to choose the right type of system for the situation, especially when it comes to loudspeakers and amplifiers.

The Role Of The Band PA

The role of a concert PA system is fairly easily understood in that it has to amplify the whole band and project the sound to fill a large auditorium, but in a club environment the PA plays more of a reinforcement role, augmenting the sound of the on-stage backline amplification as well as carrying the vocals. For example, in a typical pub gig the guitarist's amplifier is likely to produce almost enough volume, so little help is needed from the PA system. In such situations the main job of the PA is to lift the vocals over the level of the backline and drums. If space or your budget is tight, a smaller system with a less extended bass response will handle vocals perfectly adequately. However, some capacity for handling bass is useful in those gigs where the backline can't cope on its own.

Sound Control

A larger PA system provides more control over what the audience hears, and it follows that, if you want your sound engineer to have a reasonable degree of control over a mix in a small venue, it's a good idea to use modestly-powered backline amplification and then mic it up. This not only gives the mix engineer more leeway to turn things up but it also reduces the amount of spill from the backline amplifiers into the vocal mics, resulting in a clearer sound all round. Spill can be a major problem in some venues, and various strategies for improving on-stage sound is discussed elsewhere in this series of books. For typical pub gigs, guitar combo amplifiers rated at around 50 watts each and bass/keyboard amplifiers rated at around 100 watts are usually adequate. A 200-watt guitar stack used in a small venue will rob the sound engineer of virtually all control.

PA loudspeakers

The loudspeaker is one of the main components of any PA system, and both the design of the speaker and the enclosure in which it is mounted have a profound effect on the system's performance. The essential task of any loudspeaker is to convert electrical energy into acoustic energy as accurately and as efficiently as possible. Although the range of our hearing decreases with age (and with exposure to damagingly-high sound levels), the range of human hearing is usually considered to be 20Hz-20kHz, and this is generally accepted as being the frequency range over which a well-designed audio system should operate. However, the laws of physics conspire to make it very difficult for a single loudspeaker to cover the entire audio spectrum with any degree of efficiency.

To reproduce low frequencies effectively – where we

may be dealing with wavelengths of 40 feet or longer – it's necessary to move a lot of air, which is why conventional bass speakers have larger diameters than high-frequency or mid-range speakers. Another general rule is that large-diameter drivers usually require larger cabinets, which explains why bass enclosures are large and heavy.

While large-diameter speakers can reproduce low frequencies quite effectively, their high moving mass and large dimensions means that they are relatively poor at reproducing higher frequencies, so in most systems the audio range is shared between speakers of differing sizes, each handling the section of the audio spectrum to which it is best suited. Some circuitry needs to be added to route the required part of the audio spectrum to the appropriate speakers, and this is called a crossover.

Crossovers

A crossover is used to send only the relevant part of the audio spectrum to each speaker, and the spectrum may be divided into two or more frequency bands, depending on the size of the system. The simplest type of crossover comprises passive filtering circuitry and is usually built into the speaker cabinet. Electrically, the passive crossover comes between the power amplifier and the speakers. In a two-way system the bass is handled by a low-frequency driver, also known as a woofer, and the treble by a high-frequency driver, or tweeter. In larger systems there may be one or more additional speakers handling the mid range, and these are called mid-range drivers.

Drivers

A chassis loudspeaker without a box or cabinet is called a driver. The familiar cone driver comprises a stiff cone of doped paper or synthetic material suspended in a rigid cage or chassis by means of a flexible surround, as shown in Figure 1.1. The narrow end of the cone is fixed onto a parallel-sided tube, or former, onto which is wound a coil of thin wire, and the coil is positioned in a slot between the poles of a powerful magnet. When current passes through the coil a force is set up between it and the magnet, causing the cone of the driver to move either backwards or forwards from its neutral position depending on the polarity of the current. If the current passed through the coil is an audio signal then sound is produced from the cone.

The driver is fed from the output of a power amplifier, which amplifies the small audio signal from a mixing desk or some other source.

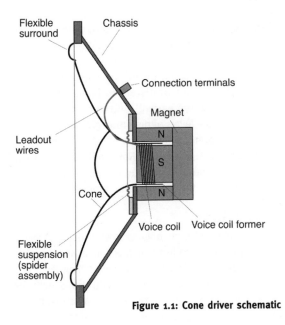

Figure 1.1: Cone driver schematic

Driver Distortion

From the above illustration it is evident that the cone can only move so far before it reaches a physical limit, at which point either the suspension will permit no more travel or the voice coil will be driven out of the gap. As the cone approaches these limits its movement becomes more restricted, so that the physical movement of the cone is no longer exactly proportional to the electrical input. The result is distortion.

All loudspeaker systems distort to some extent, but as long as the amount of distortion is kept small the human hearing system will perceive the sound as accurate. Audible levels of distortion give rise to a fuzzy or unclear sound, where musical detail and vocal intelligibility becomes lost. Note that distortion will also occur if the original audio signal has become distorted during the amplification process.

Limitations

A loudspeaker cone can only reproduce the input signal faithfully if it behaves like a rigid piston, pushing against air – if it bends or vibrates in other ways then distortion will occur, as any unwanted vibrations will be superimposed on the wanted sound. Much work has been done on researching the correct cone shape and materials to reduce distortion, but some is inevitable. After all, the basic principle of a cone driver is very crude, and all of the movement comes from magnetic forces pushing against the voice coil. This places enormous mechanical stresses on the components, and very strong adhesives are required anchor the speaker cone assembly and prevent it from literally shaking itself apart.

Another major physical limitation on the power handling of a loudspeaker is the heat generated in the voice coil. Loudspeakers are relatively inefficient devices, and most of the amplifier power fed into them is converted into heat. If more heat is generated than can be dissipated then the temperature will continue to increase and the coil will eventually burn out. Before this occurs, however, the increased temperature of the voice coil and magnet system will reduce the loudspeaker's efficiency – a phenomenon known as power compression. This is very dangerous, as the instinctive reaction of the PA operator is to increase the power in order to obtain more volume. This, as you might expect, can lead to driver failure.

Most heat is lost by radiation into the magnet and chassis metalwork, so some high-frequency devices use a liquid to fill the space, such as Ferrofluid. This is a colloidal suspension of magnetic material in a lubricating liquid which conducts heat away from the coil.

Bass Drivers

A driver required to deliver high levels of bass sounds needs to have a relatively large diameter, but the larger the cone the more rigid it has to be so that it doesn't bend or deform under load, and this in turn results in the need for a heavier cone assembly.

basic Live Sound

The mass of a large-diameter voice coil capable of handling the high energies which are encountered in PA bass applications is also significant. Simple mechanics tells us that accelerating a large mass requires far more energy than accelerating a small mass. The faster you try to move the cone the higher the inertial resistance to that movement, and in audio terms this means that the higher the frequency the harder it is to move the cone. This is one reason why large bass drivers are unable to faithfully reproduce high frequencies.

Another reason why large bass drivers can't reproduce high frequencies effectively is their diameter. If you imagine an 18-inch diameter bass driver that has somehow been built with an infinitely light, infinitely rigid cone and an infinitely powerful magnetic motor, it would seem that it should be able to function as a high-frequency driver. However, even if these impossible criteria were met, the performance of the driver would still be compromised by its geometry. The diameter of the cone would simply be too large to deal with the wavelengths of the high-frequency sounds being reproduced. While this wouldn't affect the ability of the driver to project sound forward, consider what would happen if you moved slightly to one side.

Figure 1.2: Off-axis effects

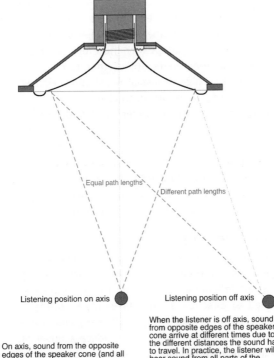

Listening position on axis

Listening position off axis

On axis, sound from the opposite edges of the speaker cone (and all points in between) arrive at essentially the same time, so no phase cancellation occurs

When the listener is off axis, sound from opposite edges of the speaker cone arrive at different times due to the different distances the sound has to travel. In practice, the listener will hear sound from all parts of the cone, all with slightly different time delays. The resulting phase cancellation will conspire to reduce the level of off-axis sounds

Figure 1.2 illustrates how sound originating from the side of the cone nearest to you will reach your ears before sound from the further side, and the same is true of all points in between. This results in phase cancellation, and the further you move away from the main axis of the loudspeaker the more serious it becomes. Large-diameter drivers therefore tend to concentrate their high-frequency output into a relatively narrow beam, whereas lower frequencies are propagated along a much wider angle of dispersion. This 'beaming' effect becomes more serious with higher frequencies, which not only prevents the system from providing an even audience coverage but also invites feedback, as it is highly likely that a reflection from one of these tightly-beamed high-frequency sounds will find its way back into a stage microphone.

Cone Breakup

Distortion also occurs at high frequencies because the cone of the driver ceases to behave as a perfect piston – it starts to vibrate, or break up. The term 'breakup' is used to describe a cone assembly vibrating or rippling under a load – it doesn't imply mechanical failure. The designer's job is to produce a driver for which there are no significant breakup problems in the frequency range within which the driver will be expected to perform.

Mid-Range And Beyond

The usual way to solve problems with driver beaming is to use loudspeakers of progressively smaller diameters to handle the higher frequencies. In other words, mid-range drivers are smaller than bass drivers, while high-frequency drivers are even smaller still.

Mid-range drivers are usually cone drivers, similar in construction to bass drivers but physically smaller, and they may be mounted in a different type of cabinet or enclosure. High-frequency drivers, on the other hand, must be small enough so that the direct radiating area may be only one or two square inches. Hi-fi tweeters often employ small dome-shaped diaphragms instead of cones, in which the diaphragm is driven by a voice-coil arrangement similar to that employed in the cone loudspeaker, although the distance of travel is very much smaller. Horn-loaded tweeters are almost always used in PA applications because they are more efficient, and they comprise a compression driver – not unlike an industrial-grade hi-fi tweeter – feeding into a flared horn.

Using a horn has two main advantages: firstly, it significantly increases acoustic efficiency by matching the driver to the air in the room more efficiently (think of it as an acoustic gearbox); secondly, the horn shape controls the directivity or angle of coverage of the sound, enabling it to be focused more precisely. If you can control the output from a tweeter to concentrate it into a narrow angle then it's reasonable to assume that you'd get a higher sound level in this way than you would from spreading the same amount of sound energy over a wider angle. This also makes it easier to array multiple cabinets at slightly different angles, thus covering a wider overall area without allowing the tweeter coverage to overlap significantly. Figure 1.3 shows both a conventional direct-radiating tweeter and a compression-driven horn.

A more recent development is the constant directivity horn, in which the profile of the horn is designed to prevent the lower end of the high-frequency part of the audio spectrum from being radiated over too wide an angle. (With a non-constant directivity system, the dispersion angle narrows as the frequency increases). This artificial tailoring of the directivity generally makes the very top end of the high-frequency band too quiet in comparison with the lower end, because it's being spread out over a larger angle, and so it's necessary for some filtering to be introduced in the crossover circuitry in order to compensate.

Horns are also often employed to increase the efficiency and to control the directivity of mid-range drivers, but because of the larger dimensions of the horn required to handle the longer wavelengths it will probably be built from wood, glass fibre or rigid foam. Horn-loaded cone driver systems are more frequently found in large sound systems used in touring than in the smaller systems that a gigging band might own.

Figure 1.3: HF driver schematic

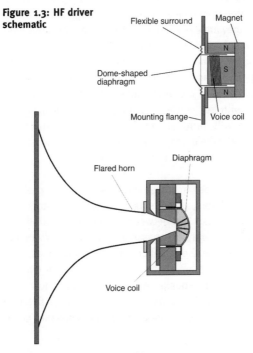

More About Crossovers

Bass driver cones move relatively slowly over quite large distances, whereas high-frequency driver diaphragms move over a more limited distance but more quickly. High-frequency drivers therefore need to be protected from potentially damaging low-frequency signals outside their range. Similarly, bass and mid drivers must be prevented from receiving frequencies higher than those which they are designed to reproduce, not because they will be damaged but to prevent high-frequency beaming. Furthermore, most drivers are only capable of producing a flat frequency response and low distortion over a specific part of the audio spectrum, and so feeding a driver with frequencies which it was never designed to handle will seriously compromise the quality and accuracy of the overall sound. This is why the crossover is such an important part of the system.

At its simplest a crossover is a series of passive electrical filters, comprising resistors, capacitors and inductive coils wired between the amplifier output and the drivers, and such passive systems are invariably located inside the speaker cabinets themselves. In a three-way system, comprising bass, mid and tweeter units, the bass speaker would be fed via a low-pass filter, which only allows through frequencies below a certain limit. This ensures that the bass speaker never has to deal with frequencies higher than those it was designed to reproduce.

A mid-range speaker has both upper and lower limits of safe operation, so it has to be fed via both high- and low-pass filters to ensure that it receives only mid-range frequencies. Frequencies which are too low will cause damage and distortion, whereas high frequencies will result in beaming and coloration.

High-frequency drivers are fed via a high-pass filter to ensure that they receive frequencies only above a certain limit, so it's important for the designer to select bass/mid and high-frequency drivers that overlap slightly in terms of the ranges they can cover to ensure a seamless crossover transition. Figure 1.4 shows how a three-way crossover splits the audio spectrum.

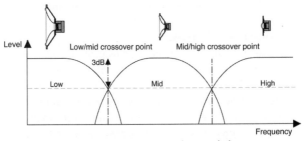

Figure 1.4: Three-way crossover characteristic

Passive Crossover Limitations

The type of crossover previously described is known as a passive crossover because the only circuitry it requires comprises passive filters. Such designs are generally reliable and inexpensive, but they are best suited only to relatively low-power applications, as some of the amplifier power is absorbed by the passive crossover circuit, resulting in a loss of efficiency, and unless all three drivers are equally efficient at turning electrical energy into acoustic energy (which is very unlikely) the more efficient drivers must be fed with attenuated or reduced signals in order to bring them down to the level of the least efficient driver in the system. In other words, power must be deliberately wasted to obtain a flat frequency response across the audio spectrum, and an accurate system must have a flat frequency response. This simply means that all frequencies within the audio range are treated equally, rather than some being amplified more than others.

Crossover Slopes

Because of the restrictions imposed by passive circuitry, the filter characteristic of a passive crossover can't be made particularly steep without wasting power and using a lot of expensive components. A filter doesn't simply block all frequencies beyond its cutoff point; instead it has a sloping response that reduces frequencies beyond the cutoff point by so many decibels per octave. The more decibels per octave the sharper the response of the filter is said to be. Simple passive filters usually have slopes of 6dB or 12dB per octave, and in practical terms this means that the drivers receive significant amounts of power outside their ideal range. For example, on a filter with a slope of 6dB per octave the signal voltage is only halved for every octave beyond the cut off point, whereas a 24dB-per-octave filter will reduce the signal to $1/16$ of the original for each octave beyond the cutoff frequency.

As well as making sure that each driver covers only its designated frequency range, a steep filter also minimises the area of overlap between drivers handling adjacent frequency bands. This is usually a good thing because a wide overlap can lead to phase problems as both drivers struggle to deliver a slightly different version of what's going on in the crossover's overlap region.

Active Crossovers

PA systems, we now know, were revolutionised by the introduction of the active crossover, a device that allows an audio signal to be split into different frequency bands before it reaches the power amplifiers. This enables separate power amplifiers to be used to drive the bass-, mid- and high-frequency loudspeakers, and

basic Live Sound

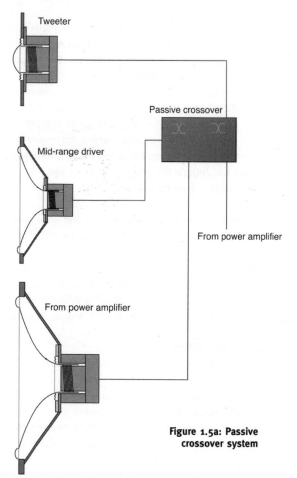

Tweeter

Passive crossover

Mid-range driver

From power amplifier

From power amplifier

**Figure 1.5a: Passive
crossover system**

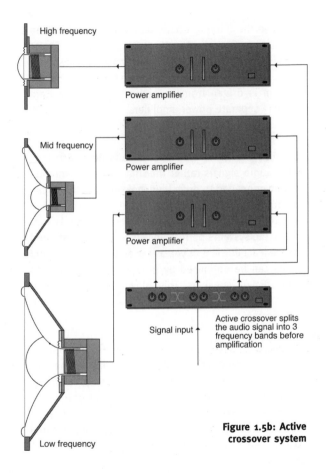

High frequency

Power amplifier

Mid frequency

Power amplifier

Power amplifier

Signal input

Active crossover splits
the audio signal into 3
frequency bands before
amplification

Low frequency

**Figure 1.5b: Active
crossover system**

because the filtering occurs before the amplifiers no amplifier power is lost in the crossover circuit. Figure 1.5a shows a simple three-way passive crossover system, while in Figure 1.5b the same three-way speaker system is driven from an active crossover system feeding separate power amplifiers.

Active Advantages

Because the active crossover circuits deal with low-level audio signals rather than the massive amounts of power needed to drive loudspeakers, the filters can be built with active electronic circuitry, allowing much greater flexibility and precision in their design. What's more, the system's performance is no longer restricted by the least efficient driver, as the amplifier powers and gains can be optimised by providing more power to less efficient speakers. This allows the designers far more flexibility when selecting drive units to be used in a system.

Active crossovers considerably reduce the risk of damage to the driver because an overload in one part of the audio spectrum won't necessarily cause an overload in the other areas. With typical pop music programme material, the energy at the bass end of the spectrum exceeds that at the high end by far, and in a passive system this can damage the tweeters.

Imagine what happens when a dance record is played so loud that the amplifier is driven into clipping distortion. The amplifier clips every time a loud bass note or drum beat is played, producing square waves rich in high-frequency harmonics. These pass through the crossover in the same way as legitimate high-frequency signals, and so they reach the tweeter. If these artificially-generated harmonics are high enough in level and long enough in duration they may cause mechanical damage or they may overheat the voice coil to such a degree that it burns out.

In the same situation in an active system, where the crossover comes before the amplifiers, an overload at the bass end will be confined to the bass amplifier. The mid-range drivers and tweeters will still receive clean signals from their own amplifiers.

Abusing Drivers

A loudspeaker has both mechanical and thermal limits beyond which damage occurs. A loudspeaker cone or tweeter diaphragm can only move a certain distance before it reaches the physical limits of the suspension system, and the voice coil (the outer edge of a loudspeaker cone) is attached to a cast or pressed metal chassis via a flexible surround, which is designed to hold the cone in a central position while impeding its movement as little as possible. The voice coil assembly at the narrow end of the cone is centred by means of a flexible corrugated surround, known as a spider, and again the degree of movement available to it is limited. If too much signal is applied to the loudspeaker either the suspension will run out of travel or the voice coil will be driven out of the magnetic gap, and as the cone approaches these limits the physical movement is no longer proportional to the electrical input because, as the suspension becomes stretched, it produces a force opposing the cone's motion. Another potential mechanical weak spot is the speaker lead-out wires – the flexible conductors joining the moving coil to the stationary connector strip or terminal on the chassis. Excessive or violent excursions of the cone can cause these to break.

If the loudspeaker is driven too hard for any length of time, mechanical damage is almost certain – if the voice coil doesn't burn out first! If the power isn't kept within safety limits the temperature of the voice coil will continue to rise until the wire melts or the heat distorts the coil former to such an extent that it rubs on the sides of the magnetic gap. A similar result occurs if the coil becomes unglued from its former. Either way, complete failure occurs soon afterwards, and the only cure is an expensive recone job.

Speaker Power Ratings

Most loudspeakers are rated on the assumption that the music fed into them will comprise loud peaks with some quieter sections in between, but the use of compressors and limiters reduces the dynamic range of the input signal by a considerable degree. Increasing the average signal level in this way means that thermal problems are more likely to arise, so the power ratings published in loudspeaker manuals can't always be taken at face value.

Other, non-thermal damage is most likely to occur when the speaker is driven with a heavily clipped signal from an under-powered amplifier. In effect the speaker will try to respond to a square wave, and the voice coil assembly, as well as heating up, can quite literally shake itself to pieces. As a general rule, speakers tolerate short periods of undistorted overload much more easily than they can withstand prolonged periods of clipped input.

Loudspeakers And Loudness

The power rating of a loudspeaker tells you just how much electrical power the speaker can handle, but it doesn't tell you how much acoustic power is produced – it doesn't tell you how much of the input power is converted into sound. Even the most efficient loudspeakers convert only a few per cent of the electrical input into sound, but there's a large difference between the most and least efficient speakers around.

A useful figure to know is the maximum sound pressure level which the speaker can produce, but this can be misleading as the figures are sometimes calculated instead of measured and often take no account of power compression. It's often better to buy a speaker by reputation rather than relying entirely on what is written on the spec sheet.

Loudspeaker Enclosures

Loudspeakers are of little use without an enclosure or cabinet, and this is fairly obvious when you consider what would happen if you tried to use a loudspeaker driver on its own, as shown in Figure 1.6. Whenever a loudspeaker cone moves forward it compresses the air directly in front of it while the air pressure behind the cone is reduced, and when it moves back the opposite happens. In the absence of an enclosure there's nothing to prevent the high-pressure air in front of the cone from simply flowing around the edge of the speaker into the low-pressure region at the rear, which is exactly what happens. In other words, instead of the acoustic energy being projected into the room

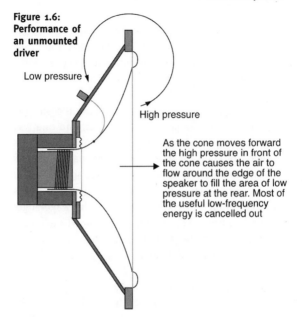

Figure 1.6: Performance of an unmounted driver

Low pressure

High pressure

As the cone moves forward the high pressure in front of the cone causes the air to flow around the edge of the speaker to fill the area of low pressure at the rear. Most of the useful low-frequency energy is cancelled out

by the loudspeaker driver, a lot of the energy produced is wasted.

The lower the frequency the more time the air has to move around the edge of the speaker before the cone changes direction, which means that, at bass frequencies, virtually all of the energy is wasted in pumping air from the front of the driver to the back and vice versa. In effect, instead of generating a sound wave that can be projected into the room, the driver creates a localised pocket of turbulence, with radiated sound as a by-product.

What's needed is some way of stopping the air from leaking around the sides of the driver, and one way of achieving this is by mounting it on a baffle, as shown in Figure 1.7 on the next page. In this illustration, a driver is shown mounted in a cutout at the centre of a large flat plate, or baffle. If the baffle is large enough in comparison with the wavelength of the low-frequency sound, the air won't have time to move from the front of the baffle to the back before the cone changes direction.

Assuming that no sound actually passes through the baffle, all of the sound generated at the rear of the speaker cone is wasted as far as the listener in front of the speaker is concerned. A huge baffle isn't a practical way of mounting loudspeakers for live performance, and so the next logical step is to fold the baffle into the shape of a box and then use absorbent material inside the box to soak up the unwanted power from the rear of the driver. This is known as an infinite baffle enclosure. Such a box may have to be fairly large to obtain a good low-frequency

**Figure 1.7: Driver
fitted to flat baffle**

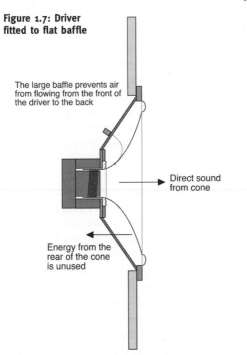

The large baffle prevents air
from flowing from the front of
the driver to the back

Direct sound
from cone

Energy from the
rear of the cone
is unused

response, and the acoustic efficiency isn't great
because half of the sound energy is absorbed inside
the box. When the front of the cone couples directly
with the air in the room, instead of feeding a horn
flare, it is known as a direct radiator.

PA Enclosures

When using a portable PA it's generally desirable to generate as much acoustic energy as possible from the smallest practical enclosure, and this usually means choosing an electrically-efficient driver and mounting it in a ported or vented enclosure, an example of which is shown in Figure 1.8. The type of enclosure shown here is a direct-radiating ported system. The port causes the box to resonate at a certain frequency, like a milk bottle resonates at a fixed note when you blow over its neck. If the enclosure/port is tuned so that this 'note' occurs at the point at which the natural bass end of the speaker starts to roll off, the bass response can usefully be extended downwards by making constructive use of the energy normally absorbed by the box. The frequency of resonance depends on the volume of air inside, the dimensions of the port and the mechanical springiness of the loudspeaker. Damping the box is another trick used often to widen the frequency range at which the box resonates, stopping it from sounding too boomy. It's very important not to feed frequencies into ported loudspeaker enclosures that are below the cutoff frequency of the cabinet because, below the resonant frequency of the box, the air in the cabinet no longer loads the speaker cone. Without an air load against which it can push, the cone is free to move to the limits of its mechanical excursion, where damage can occur.

Figure 1.8: Ported enclosure

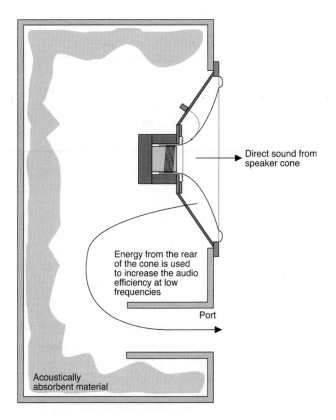

Direct sound from
speaker cone

Energy from the rear
of the cone is used
to increase the audio
efficiency at low
frequencies

Port

Acoustically
absorbent material

Horn Loading

Even with the benefits of porting, direct-radiating loudspeaker systems are relatively inefficient. Loudspeaker cones are very effective at pushing hard against small volumes of air, but what we actually want in this case is to move a large volume of air over a short distance. Transferring energy from a moving driver cone to the air in an efficient manner involves mechanical matching, and this can be significantly improved by placing the driver at the end of an exponential horn. This type of enclosure is used in larger systems to increase the efficiency of bass and mid enclosures. Horns can also be used to control the directivity of mid-range speakers for those situations in which it's necessary to use a number of cabinets in an array. However, bass and mid horns aren't particularly well suited for use with portable PA systems, so I won't be examining their operation in any depth here. High-frequency horns, on the other hand, are used in virtually all PA systems.

Compact PA

The type of PA system most commonly used for small gigs is built around compact two- or three-way integrated speaker cabinets, in which the bass end is generally handled by a 12- or 15-inch loudspeaker and the high end by a horn-loaded compression driver. Three-way systems may have a direct-radiating or shallow horn-loaded mid-range driver, and both active and passive systems are available. For systems rated at a few hundred watts, passive crossovers provide an inexpensive and technically acceptable solution, and one power amplifier is required to drive the cabinet rather than the two or three needed for an active system.

Unfortunately, conventional active systems have significant amount of wiring between the crossovers, power amps and speaker cabinets, which is probably one of the reasons why more manufacturers are building integrated active systems in which the crossover and power amps are fitted inside the speaker cabinet. This would obviously be impractically heavy for most large concert systems, but for smaller systems it provides a very convenient solution. A number of manufacturers have used moulded plastic cabinets to house such systems, often formed into complex shapes, but although these shapes may be acoustically beneficial it can be difficult to stack the cabinets during transportation.

Multiple Driver Cabinets

Some manufacturers use a number of identical small-diameter drivers in compact full-range systems, and the most well-known example is probably the Bose 802. If a driver is physically small in diameter it can cover a very wide frequency range, which is why small radios,

TV sets and similar domestic audio products can produce audio of reasonable quality with just a single speaker. Advances in technology means that relatively powerful small speakers can now be built, and if a number of these are used they can handle sufficient power for small and medium-sized PA applications. The bass doesn't go as deep it does as with a dedicated bass bin, and the top end doesn't extend quite as high as it does with a good tweeter, so pre-EQ may be required from a processing box designed to flatten the response of the speakers, which can lead to a lowering of low-frequency headroom. Over the normal vocal range, however, such systems can perform exceptionally well. Apart from their lack of headroom at the bass end of the audio spectrum, they are also often less efficient than conventionally-designed speakers, and consequently a large power amplifier is required to drive them. At one time this could have been a problem, but high-power amplifiers are now less heavy and less expensive than they used to be.

Sub-bass In Small Systems

In those cases where more bass power is needed, and where bass reproduction is required to extend to a lower frequency than compact PA cabinets can manage, you could either use larger full-range cabinets (which isn't really practical if you're touring in a hatchback) or you could add one or more sub-bass speakers to your existing compact system. The principle is the same whether the existing speakers use multiple small-diameter drivers or conventional bass/mid drivers augmented by horns.

Because of the long wavelengths involved in reproducing bass sounds it's possible to position the bass speakers away from the mid/high boxes without compromising the sound significantly. Furthermore, because low frequencies are essentially omni-directional in nature it's possible to use just a single mono sub-bass cabinet as part of a stereo system without losing the stereo image. For such a system to work effectively, however, a crossover must be used to remove bass frequencies from the mid/high feed and to remove mid and high frequencies from the sub-bass feed. Depending on the system, this may be achieved by using passive crossovers located within the sub-bass cabinet itself or by means of a two-way active crossover and separate power amplifiers. If only a single sub-bass speaker is used it will be necessary to use an active crossover that can provide a mono sub-bass output, and of course additional amplification will be needed for any sub-bass enclosure fed from an active crossover.

If possible, the sub-bass speaker or speakers should be placed in line with the main speakers to keep the two sound sources time-aligned with each other. If the bass speaker is placed a long way in front of the satellite speakers the bass energy will arrive before the rest of the sound, whereas placing the bass speakers too far back will cause the bass to be delayed. The seriousness of this problem depends on the acoustics of the room and on the crossover frequency being used, but it's good practice to keep the alignment as accurate as possible.

Mounting a sub-bass speaker close to a solid wall and on the floor will increase the amount of bass that can be obtained from the system due to an effect known as the boundary effect. At very low frequencies a bass speaker emits sound in all directions, and if the cabinet is standing away from the wall the sound emitted from the rear of the cabinet will reflect from the wall and then combine with the sound coming from the front of the cabinet. Because it takes some time for the sound to reach the wall and bounce back again, it will be out of phase with the direct sound at some frequencies, causing cancellation. The outcome is a loss of energy at some frequencies, resulting in an uneven bass.

If the bass speaker is placed close to the wall, all of the reflected sound from the rear of the cabinet will be very nearly in phase with the sound from the front of the speaker, resulting in an overall increase in bass level. Standing sub-bass cabinets in corners can produce a further rise in bass efficiency because the sound then reflects from two walls. This dodge can sometimes help to squeeze a little more out of a marginal system if you're short on power, although it may sometimes result in a bass end that is more boomy than usual.

Power Amplifiers

Because clipped signals pose a far greater threat to a loudspeaker than short, undistorted signal peaks exceeding the speaker's nominal power rating, it's safer to have too much amplifier power at your disposal than too little as there will be less likelihood of clipping distortion. Possibly the best arrangement is to have an amplifier capable of delivering between 25% and 50% more power than your speakers require, but a limiter should be used to ensure that the amplifier can never be driven into clipping. Obviously, if you have an amplifier rated at a higher power than your speakers and you still manage to drive it into clipping you're almost certainly going to damage your speakers, so you need some way of preventing this. Some amplifiers are now available with built-in limiting, and this strikes me as a very good idea.

Fan cooling is recommended for powers of greater than around 200 watts per channel, although there are some new designs of amplifier that work more efficiently than conventional designs which make fan cooling unnecessary. A regular class A/B power amplifier dissipates almost as much power in heat as it delivers to the speakers, so a 600-watt amplifier working hard might leave you with 400-500 watts of waste heat of which you'll need to dispose. That's around half the power output of an electric fire bar, so you can see why good ventilation is essential. Leaving spaces between power amplifiers in racks is a good idea, and you should be careful not to position any heat-sensitive equipment directly above a power amplifier.

Active Crossover Facilities

Active crossovers are connected before the power amplifier, so they handle only line level signals, no matter how powerful the system. This means that conventional active circuitry can be used, and because electronic components of this type are relatively cheap it's possible to build many more features into the crossover. For example, it may be possible to adjust the crossover frequencies, select different crossover slopes and adjust the gain of the various bands as well as to provide integral limiting. Other common features include a mono sub-bass output, individual band delays for time-alignment and equalisation for constant-directivity horns.

Because the performance of the crossover is independent of the load's impedance characteristics, the same active device can be used with a number of different types of loudspeaker. Also, any clipping caused by the power amplifier will affect only the speaker connected to that power amplifier, so a distorting bass end won't put the tweeters in jeopardy.

2 MICROPHONES

A wide range of dynamic and capacitor microphones are used in the recording studio, but in most live sound applications – especially at the lower end of the market – dynamic mics are the most commonly-used model because of their affordability and robust construction. However, there are capacitor and back-electret capacitor microphones that offer advantages in certain live applications, and some are surprisingly cheap.

Impedance

Microphones are generally available in high-impedance unbalanced or low-impedance balanced varieties. Virtually all professional audio equipment uses the low-impedance balanced format, and if your microphone connects via a three-pin XLR at the base of the body it almost certainly falls into this category. Conversely, a mic with a fixed cable terminating in a single-pole jack plug is likely to be high impedance unbalanced. High-impedance mics are used mainly with older all-in-one mixer amplifiers, and cable lengths should not exceed 15 feet or so with this variety or the high end will suffer and interference may become a problem. Low-impedance balanced mics, however, can be used with much longer cables with no loss of signal quality.

Dynamic Microphones

Dynamic mics are relatively inexpensive, mechanically robust, and require no electrical power to operate, which makes them attractive for both recording and live-sound applications. At the heart of the dynamic microphone is a rigid, lightweight diaphragm attached to a coil of extremely thin insulated wire. This coil is suspended within a magnetic field created by a permanent magnet, much like a loudspeaker voice coil, and as the diaphragm assembly moves backwards and forwards in response to sound a small electrical current is generated. Because the diaphragm is moving in response to sonic vibrations the output signal is a direct electrical representation of that sound. The diaphragm, voice coil and magnetic assembly are incorporated into a single unit, known as the microphone capsule, and this is usually visible if the protective wire basket is removed.

The sound energy must move both the microphone's diaphragm and the coil which is attached to it, and because the assembly has a measurable mass any increase in the speed of its movement is countered by its own inertia. Inertia resists acceleration, and a

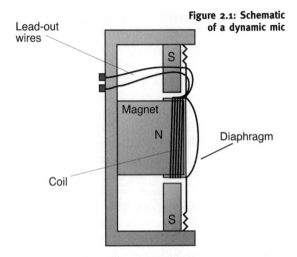

Figure 2.1: Schematic of a dynamic mic

Lead-out wires

S

Magnet

N

Diaphragm

Coil

S

vibrating microphone diaphragm has to accelerate and decelerate many times each second as the diaphragm moves first one way and then the other. In practice this places an upper-frequency limit on dynamic mics of around 16kHz, though some ingenious designs have managed to push this figure a little higher. Figure 2.1 shows the schematic of a typical dynamic microphone.

Dynamic Efficiency
A dynamic microphone is really just a tiny electricity generator in which the sound source provides the

power, but because the amount of sound energy reaching the microphone is so small the electrical output is also very limited, and the signal must therefore be amplified many times before it is large enough to be usable. The more a signal is amplified the more electrical background noise is added, which means that, when working with quiet or distant sound sources, dynamic microphones can run into noise problems. However, for most situations involving PAs, the sound sources are relatively loud and usually quite close to the microphones.

Capacitor Microphones

Capacitor microphones, sometimes known as condenser microphones, are generally considered to be the most accurate type of microphone because they are able to respond to very high audio frequencies and they can be made to be sensitive enough to work with quiet or more distant sound sources. Capacitor microphones don't have voice coils but they still need a diaphragm, although this can be much thinner and lighter than that in a dynamic mic, which is why the microphone can respond more effectively to a range of high frequencies.

As the diaphragm vibrates, its distance from the stationary metal plate varies accordingly, and if a fixed

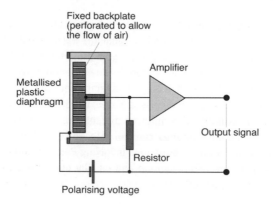

Fixed backplate
(perforated to allow
the flow of air)

Amplifier

Metallised
plastic
diaphragm

Output signal

Resistor

Polarising voltage

Figure 2.2: Schematic of a capacitor mic

electrical charge is applied between the diaphragm and
the plate a corresponding change in electrical voltage
is produced. This change in voltage is then amplified
by circuitry within the microphone, which is why
capacitor microphones need electrical power in order
to operate. Power is also needed to provide the
electrical charge on the diaphragm, as can be seen in
Figure 2.2.

Capacitor mics are much more sensitive than dynamic
models and have a better high-end frequency response,
but they are usually more expensive and less robust.

Electret Mics

An electret mic is a type of capacitor microphone in which the diaphragm contains a permanent electrical charge sealed in an insulating material rather than relying on an external power source, and Figure 2.3 shows an internal schematic. A pre-amplifier is still required within the microphone, but this may be battery operated in some models, which is useful in those situations where phantom power is not available. However, the majority of professional electret mics can also operate on phantom power when required.

Originally, electret mics weren't particularly good performers because a diaphragm that could hold a magnetic charge was also much thicker and heavier

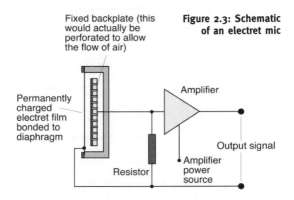

Fixed backplate (this would actually be perforated to allow the flow of air)

Figure 2.3: Schematic of an electret mic

Amplifier

Permanently charged electret film bonded to diaphragm

Output signal

Amplifier power source

Resistor

than that on a true capacitor model. As a result, they had limited sensitivity and a rather poor high-frequency response.

Back-Electret Mics

Fixing the permanently-charged material to the capsule's stationary backplate rather than to the diaphragm was a simple concept which allowed electret mics to use the same lightweight diaphragms used by conventional capacitor models, hence the term 'back electret'. The best back-electret mic can rival a conventional capacitor microphone in all aspects of performance, and often at a much lower cost. Figure 2.4 describes how a back-electret microphone works.

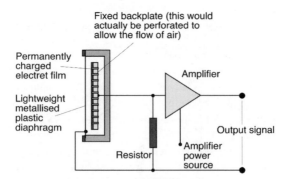

Figure 2.4: Schematic of a back-electret mic

Polar Patterns

Omnidirectional microphones pick up sound equally well from any direction. However, this isn't always ideal – it's sometimes useful to have the microphone pick up sound more selectively. These days, microphones are available with a wide range of directional characteristics, the most common for use in live situations being the cardioid, or unidirectional, polar pattern.

Dynamic mics, along with most back-electret mics, are available only with fixed pickup patterns, but some capacitor mics use a dual diaphragm capsule construction so that the polar pattern may be changed by means of a switch. These are most often found in studios, but some models are favoured for specific stage applications.

Cardioid Patterns

Unidirectional microphones pick up sound from mainly one direction. This type of microphone is commonly referred to as a cardioid microphone because a graph of its sensitivity is approximately heart shaped at different angles. Because the cardioid microphone is most effective when picking up sounds from in front, it helps to exclude spill from backline and stage monitors and also helps to reduce the risk of

basic Live Sound

Figure 2.5: Main polar patterns

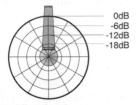

Omnidirectional:
Picks up sound equally from all directions. Used mainly for recording or for picking up multiple sound sources at the same time

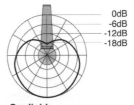

Cardioid:
Picks up sound mainly from the front. Least sensitive at the rear, making it a good choice for live performance

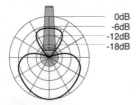

Hypercardioid:
Sometimes called a supercardioid, this is a narrower pattern than the cardioid but is more sensitive to sounds coming directly from behind. Care should be taken to place monitors in the mic's dead zone

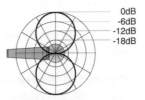

Figure of Eight:
This pattern picks up sound both from the front and rear of the capsule but not from the sides. Note that the capsule is mounted sideways, so the side of the microphone, not the end, must be aimed at the sound source

encountering feedback. A very important fact to remember about cardioid microphones is that they operate by sensing the pressure difference, or gradient, between the front of the microphone and a series of small holes, or ports, at the rear of the capsule. If you hold the mic too close to the basket you risk obscuring these ports, which will affect the directional characteristics and also increase the risk of encountering feedback.

Several versions of the cardioid pattern are available, depending on whether a narrow or wide pickup angle is required. A wide cardioid pattern may be useful if the singer moves around relative to the mic, but a wider pattern inevitably means a little more spill from other sound sources. A narrower cardioid setting, known as either hypercardioid or supercardioid, can be produced for use in situations where spill from the sides is a potential problem, but the tradeoff here is that the mic is no longer most insensitive at the rear. Figure 2.5 shows that the hypercardioid mic has a significant area of sensitivity to its rear, and its least sensitive spot is around 45° from its rear axis. It's important to know the characteristics of microphones as stage monitors must be placed in the microphones' blind spots, which for a cardioid mic is directly behind and for a hypercardioid mic is slightly to one side.

The Proximity Effect

All cardioid mics exhibit the proximity effect, which results in a significant bass boost when the microphone is used to pick up sound sources closer than a couple of inches. The closer the sound source is to the mic the more bass boost is created, and although the reason for this is rather complicated it's essentially because of the relationship between the front of the mic and the rear ports that control its directionality. If used creatively the proximity effect can provide an experienced vocalist with a way of adding tone and expression to a performance, but bad microphone technique can result in a constantly-changing tonality.

Other Pickup Patterns

Omni-pattern microphones pick up sound equally well in all directions, and because they don't rely on rear ports, they are generally more accurate than cardioid microphones. However, if they're used on stage in a live situation, they may pick up unwanted sounds, and you may also find that there's a greater likelihood of encountering feedback.

The figure-of-eight-pattern mic is equally sensitive at both the front and the back, but the sides are completely insensitive.

Frequency Characteristics

A perfectly accurate mic would have a flat frequency response, but sometimes it's more helpful to use a mic with a deliberate degree of treble boost or presence to help vocals cut through a mix. This tailoring of the mic's response, often know as adding a presence peak, is one of the factors that accounts for the reason why various models of microphone sound different.

Although the frequency response of dynamic mics isn't as good as that of capacitor mics, they tend to deliver a more punchy vocal sound that cuts through very well in a live situation. They are also useful for miking drums, guitar amps and brass instruments. Dynamic mics with extended low-frequency responses or pronounced bass-boost characteristics are also useful for miking kick drums and bass guitar amps.

Handling Noise

Hand-held microphones invariably produce some handling noise, and this varies from one model to another. One source of noise is the cable itself, and with cheap or poorly-designed mic leads you may find that bending the cable produces audible crunching noises. If this is the case, you should change your cable for a better one.

A great deal of handling noise can be eliminated by practising good mic technique, such as gripping the mic firmly and – if cable-borne rumble is a problem – holding a loop of cable in the hand along with the microphone. Low-frequency noise can also be transmitted up the mic stand from the stage, so it's a good idea to leave the desk's low cut filter switched on.

Direct Injection

When using a microphone the quality of your results will depend on both the quality of the mic and on the acoustic environment in which it is used, which on stage is noisy. Most electronic musical instruments and electric guitars and basses can be recorded by using a method known as DIing, or direct injection. This involves plugging a signal from an electronic or electric musical instrument into a mixing system, often via some form of pre-amplifier or matching transformer. Because no mic is used there's no possibility of spill and less risk of acoustic feedback, although acoustic guitars with pickups still sometimes present some feedback problems.

Radio Microphones

Just a few years ago radio mics were either prohibitively expensive or they performed very poorly. These days, however, it's possible to buy a respectable VHF system for little more than the cost of a good wired mic. VHF radio mics comprise a microphone with either an integrated transmitter or a separate belt pack, and the signal is picked up by a remote receiver, the output of which feeds into the PA in the same way as a regular mic. Special transmitter packs are available for use with guitars, and a separate receiver is needed for each radio mic.

VHF (Very High Frequency) systems are relatively cheap, and in most countries they don't require a special licence, although the number of VHF mics that can reliably work together is generally accepted to be no more than three. VHF systems are also more susceptible to interference from outside sources, such as taxi radio systems. More VHF channels can be obtained by mixing regulated and deregulated frequencies, but in some countries you will have to buy a licence in order to use the extra regulated channels.

UHF (Ultra-High-Frequency) systems are rather more expensive than VHF systems, and they may also be licensed in some countries, but with them it's possible to run more channels at the same time, and their immunity to radio-frequency interference is significantly better than that of VHF, especially in crowded suburban areas. UHF antennae are also very short, and therefore don't interfere with clothing when body packs are being used.

If you only play the occasional gig in a pub then a VHF system is the more cost-effective solution, and the occasional breakthrough of a taxi's radio signal probably won't be the end of the world. On the other hand, professionals need to be confident that taxis and radio hams won't be joining in on the choruses, and they often need more than three radio mics on the go at one time, in which case UHF is the best answer. With a UHF system it's possible to use up to four or five mics per band, and as their price continues to fall they will probably soon replace VHF systems altogether. Developments are also being made on digital radio mic systems, which should soon be able to offer even more channels, along with better immunity to interference.

A typical radio mic system will use battery-powered transmitters, although most will only accept conventional alkaline batteries and not rechargeables. Some models will work with rechargeables, but the unpredictable nature of nicad batteries means that they may run out in the middle of a show. The life of a battery is usually between one and two shows, though some systems claim up to twelve hours' use from a set of batteries.

A microphone with an integral transmitter will have a longer body than its wired counterpart, and its body will also include the battery compartment and a small stub of an aerial or antenna. Guitar versions have a guitar input jack on the body pack transmitter, generally accompanied by a sensitivity control. UHF systems are physically similar and are operated by the user in the same way.

Receivers

VHF receivers come in either normal or diversity versions, and the diversity option is strongly recommended. Inside buildings radio waves rebound from walls, causing occasional dead spots where the signal from the microphone doesn't reach the receiver with enough strength. A regular receiver has a single antenna, and if the signal fails your sound is lost.

A true diversity system has two antennae and two receiver front ends, and is fitted with a circuit that constantly switches to the antenna with the strongest signal. Because the antennae are spaced some distance apart, the chances are that one will always receive a viable signal, and so the reliability of receiving a strong signal is much improved. Cheaper diversity systems use a switching matrix to select the strongest signal from one of two antennae, whereas a true diversity system comprises two separate receivers in the same box, each of which is fed from its own antenna.

Radio Practicalities

Once the receiver has been set to the same channel as the transmitter it should be possible to switch on both transmitter and receiver to test the system. LEDs (or some other form of metering) show the RF signal strength, and on a diversity receiver there should also be LEDs to indicate which of the two receiver circuits is active. When setting up a system like this don't put the receiver too close to walls, and try to arrange things so that your normal playing position isn't less than around eight feet from the receiver or you may run into problems caused by too much signal.

To prevent the signal from breaking up when you move out of range there's usually a control known as 'squelch' which sets a threshold so that the system will mute before the signal strength drops far enough to leave your audiences listening to amplified static.

Amplifying Acoustic Guitars

Miking the acoustic guitar in the conventional manner can prove to be problematic because the high gains which are required invariably lead to problems involving feedback. The use of a good pickup will often produce better results, but it won't eliminate the risk of encountering feedback altogether. Sound picked up from the PA will cause the body of the guitar to vibrate, and these vibrations then affect the strings, which in turn feed a signal back into the pickup. Above a certain signal level the conditions for feedback reappear. You may have noticed that, when an acoustic guitar feeds back, it does so at the resonant frequency of the wooden body, whereas open vocal microphones simply squeal. Using a graphic equaliser in this situation to pull back the offending frequencies will allow you to work at a higher level, but the tone of the guitar is also likely to be affected.

Where budgets allow, personal anti-feedback systems are very effective in controlling this problem when the guitar level needs to be relatively loud. These devices work by automatically creating filter notches at those frequencies at which feedback occurred during the soundcheck.

3 MIXERS AND EQ

If you're not already familiar with mixing consoles, there are two other books in this series – *basic Mixers* and *basic Mixing Techniques* – which deal with them specifically.

The PA mixer

At its simplest, a PA system comprises loudspeaker cabinets, power amplifiers and some means of mixing several microphone signals to feed those amplifiers. This function is handled by the mixing console or, in the case of a combined mixer/amplifier, by the pre-amp section of mixer amplifier. A PA mixer doesn't have to be complex, but it should at least be fitted with basic tone controls and should have the provision to connect external effects units and signal processors, such as equalisers, limiters and so on, and it's also desirable for it to have some means of feeding a stage monitoring system. As a rule, even fairly basic stand-alone mixers will come equipped with more comprehensive features than the mixer sections present on most mixer amplifiers.

Gain Structure

Distortion will result if an electronic signal exceeds the level at which it can be accommodated by the mixer circuitry, while if the signal falls too far below this level the amount of amplification required to bring it back up to a usable level will also make it noisy. Mixer circuitry is designed to work within a particular range of signal levels, usually between one and ten volts or thereabouts. Line-level signals – such as the outputs from effects units, electronic instruments, tape machines and suchlike – are already within this range, but the signal produced by a mic may measure only a few thousandths of a volt.

Because not all microphones produce the same level of output, and because their output level depends on the proximity and loudness of the sound being recorded, the microphone amplifier is equipped with a gain control to determine the amount of amplification applied to the signal.

The simplest way of setting gain trim is to set the channel and output faders at their unity gain positions (at the odB mark, about three quarters of the way up) and then feed in the loudest signal you're likely to encounter. After this, adjust the gain trim so that the signal is just going into the red on the output meters and you're done. An alternative method, using the console's PFL buttons (if you have them), will be described later in the chapter.

Phantom Power

All capacitor mics need an electrical voltage to charge the capsule, while both capacitor and electret microphones use built-in pre-amplifiers, which also need power. Valve microphones, because of their high current consumption, require special power supply units, but the cost and fragility of these devices means that they are seldom used in live situations. Most capacitor and back-electret mics are designed to operate on phantom power, as are many active DI boxes. Phantom power is a standardised microphone powering system which passes a DC current, from a mixer's or mic pre-amp's phantom power supply, along the conductors of a balanced microphone cable. The standard voltage of a phantom power supply is 48v, and this is generated within the mixing console.

As long as a balanced microphone cable is used it's necessary only to plug in the mic and turn on the phantom power supply. Dynamic microphones do not require phantom power but they will still operate normally if it is applied, as long as they are balanced and wired via a balanced cable. If you intend to use both dynamic and capacitor mics in the same gig, with a console that has only global phantom power switching, it's vital that you check that all cables are balanced and that all mics are internally wired for balanced operation. As a rule, a mic is balanced if its body is fitted with a three-pin XLR socket.

WARNING! Using unbalanced cables or unbalanced mics with phantom power applied will compromise the sound and may damage the mics.

Mute Automation

Mute automation systems have been fitted to studio consoles for some years, but they can also be very handy in live situations, especially if you're working in a venue with two or more bands and you need to change the setup of the desk during the changeover. For example, you could arrange the desk so that all of the channels are muted except those needed by the first band and then store this setup to be recalled later. If you then do the same for the other bands, changing mix setups becomes a matter of simply pressing one or two buttons rather than resetting the whole desk.

Digital consoles that offer snapshot automation are even better, as the status of the entire console can be saved and then recalled when necessary. Even if you prefer to mix manually, automation can at least call up the correct starting conditions – including effects settings – for different bands, or even for different songs within a set.

Pink Noise

Because the majority of venues are acoustically imperfect, it's often desirable to equalise the PA feed to compensate for the worst of the room resonances. This is often achieved by feeding pink noise (a random signal containing an equal amount of energy per octave) into the speaker system and then checking the shape of the frequency response using a spectrum analyser. In this way a graphic equaliser can then be set up to 'notch out' any room resonances which may cause problems.

Talkback

Talkback is a means by which the engineer can plug a microphone into the mixer (via a designated talkback mic input) and then communicate with other members of the crew or the band via the mixer's various outputs. For example, the engineer could talk into the stage wedge monitor mix via the aux sends to communicate with the band. Talkback is rarely used with smaller PA systems, however.

Basics Of Equalisation

Although it's true that equalisers all perform essentially the same function, there's a great deal of difference between a simple two-band treble/bass tone control and a multiband studio equaliser. The simplest form of equaliser is the shelving equaliser, which is a device that applies cut or boost in much the same manner as a volume control, although it only applies it to the frequencies above or below the cutoff point set on the equaliser, depending on whether the equaliser is based around either a high-pass or a low-pass filter.

A low-pass shelving filter, as its name suggests, passes all frequencies below its cutoff frequency but attenuates

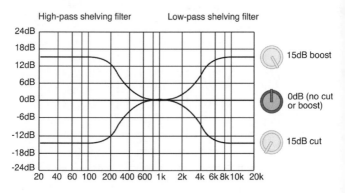

Figure 3.1: Shelving filter response

those above its cutoff frequency. Similarly, a high-pass filter passes all frequencies above its cutoff frequency but affects those below its cutoff frequency. Figure 3.1 describes the frequency response graphs of a typical treble/bass EQ using high- and low-pass filters.

Bandpass Filters

A filter that passes frequencies between two limits is known as a bandpass filter – on a mixer with a mid-range control, the mid knob controls a bandpass filter. On a typical mixer the bandpass filter will have variable cut and boost settings, and on more flexible mixers it

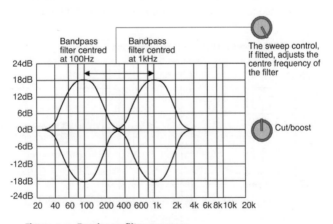

Figure 3.2: Bandpass filter response

will also be tunable so that its centre frequency can be altered. This is known as a sweep equaliser because, although the filter frequency can be changed, the width of the filter cannot. Figure 3.2 shows a typical bandpass filter response, including sweep control function. On a typical mixer the high and low shelving equalisers are used to control the high and low end, with a bandpass filter controlling the mid range.

Parametric EQ

A parametric EQ is very similar to a sweep bandpass EQ, with the addition of a third control to allow the width of the filter response to be adjusted. The width of a filter response is sometimes described as its 'Q' value, where Q is calculated by dividing the value of the filter's frequency by that of its bandwidth. High Q values are useful when picking out sounds that occupy a very narrow part of the audio spectrum, whereas lower Q values produce a smoother, more musical sound.

A studio parametric EQ may have several filter sections, enabling three or four parts of the frequency spectrum to be treated simultaneously. It can be a time-consuming process to properly set up a parametric EQ, but they are the most powerful and most flexible of the conventional types of EQ. Figure 3.3 shows a typical parametric equaliser response.

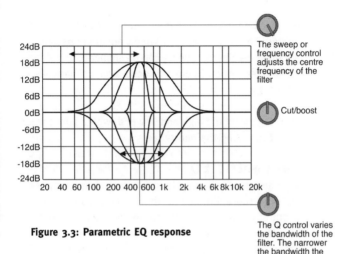

Figure 3.3: Parametric EQ response

Graphic Equalisers

A graphic equaliser is easily recognisable by the row of faders across its front panel, each of which controls a narrow section of the audio spectrum. For example, a 30-band graphic equaliser provides independent control over 30 different bands, spaced a third of an octave apart.

Other than the highest and lowest faders (which control shelving filters), each of the filters in a graphic equaliser is a fixed-frequency bandpass filter, where boost is applied when the fader is moved up from its centre position and where cut is achieved when it is moved down. Figure 3.4 shows the response of typical a graphic equaliser.

Graphic equalisers are used extensively in live sound situations to tame wayward acoustics by cutting those frequencies which aggravate room resonances, and they're also used to pull back those frequency bands in which feedback or ringing is occurring. Separate graphic equalisers are generally employed on the monitor system, where feedback is a particular problem, although they may also be built into integrated PA powered mixers.

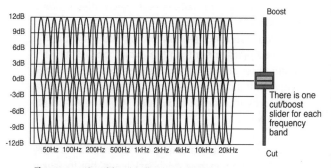

Figure 3.4: Graphic equaliser response

To Cut Or Boost?

Generally speaking, the less EQ boost you use, the more natural the final sound will be. The human ear is far more tolerant of EQ cut than it is of boost, so rather than adding lots of top end to vulnerable sounds, such as vocals, in order to get them to sit at the front of the mix, you could instead try applying high-end cut to other sounds in the mix that are conflicting with the sound in question. Furthermore, EQ boost increases the risk of encountering feedback at the boosted frequency.

Multicores

Unless the mixer is on stage with you for self operation, you are likely to need a multicore to feed the mic signals from the stage to the console. A multicore is simply a bunch of small-diameter mic cables inside a common protective outer sheath, and it's important that you use the type which contains individually-screened pairs rather than that which only provides a single outer screen for all of the cables. At the stage end, the multicore (or snake, as it is sometimes known) terminates in a metal box, upon which XLR sockets are mounted.

At the mixer end, a small multicore may simply terminate in a bunch of flying jack leads, but for larger systems it's common practice to fit a multipin connector to the end of the cable and the mating half of the connector onto the bottom of the mixer's flight case.

A separate cable or multicore (depending on the complexity of the system) is recommended to take the mixer's main and foldback outputs back to the stage for connection to the power amplifiers. Power amplifiers should always be set up as close to the speakers as possible in order to minimise the length of speaker cable used, which means that quite long signal cables may be required.

4 EFFECTS AND PROCESSORS

Along with mixers, loudspeakers, amplifiers and microphones, PA systems also usually incorporate external devices for processing signals or for adding effects, such as reverb or echo. The following chapter examines the principles and applications of all of the common types of processor and effect and how best to use them.

Compressors

Compressors and limiters are vital components of the live sound audio chain, but there's a lot of confusion concerning what they actually do. Sound balance is often at the mercy of untrained singers with less-than-perfect microphone techniques, so even if the backline you're using is perfectly balanced, you could still find that the vocal level is fluctuating all over the place. The simple cure is to keep one hand on the fader and ride the gain, but you'll always respond too late because you can't start to move the fader until you hear the problem, by which time your audience will have heard it too.

Basics Of Compression

A compressor performs essentially the same task as manual gain riding, but it does it both quickly and automatically. The aim of compression is to reduce the difference in level between the loudest and quietest sounds. The compressor monitors its own output level by electronic means to find out what the levels are doing, although some designs monitor the input level. The part of the circuit that monitors the signal level is called the side chain, and it follows the envelope of the audio signal. This level is then compared to a fixed threshold level, which is set by the user, and when the signal exceeds the threshold the side chain generates

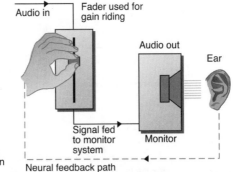

Audio in — Fader used for gain riding

Audio out

Ear

The brain monitors the signal via the ears and instructs the hand to move the fader when necessary

Signal fed to monitor system

Monitor

Neural feedback path

Figure 4.1: Manual gain riding

a control signal to reduce the signal gain using a VCA (Voltage-Controlled Amplifier). Figure 4.1 shows the simplified block diagram of a typical compressor.

Compressor Controls

The level above which the compressor decides to turn the gain down is known as the threshold. The level of gain reduction depends on the compressor's ratio control. Typically, this is variable from 1:1 (no effect at all) to infinity:1, where the output level is never allowed to rise above the threshold. The higher the ratio, the more gain reduction is applied to signals exceeding the threshold. Figure 4.2 shows a graph of the input versus the output of a compressor set for different ratio settings.

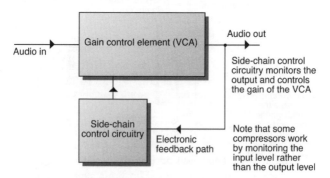

Figure 4.2: Basic compressor block diagram

Soft-Knee Compression

For those applications where less obtrusive compression is required, the soft-knee compressor may prove more useful. The main difference between a soft-knee and a conventional compressor is that, in the case of a soft-knee device, the gain is reduced progressively, starting a few decibels below the threshold, instead of everything happening as soon as the signal hits the threshold. Not all soft-knee compressors have a ratio control, however; some are completely automatic, which means that the degree of compression can be controlled by a single knob.

Attack And Release

Unless the compressor is fitted with an auto attack and release function it will probably be fitted with both attack and release time controls. Attack sets the reaction time of the compressor (how long the device takes to respond when a sound exceeds the threshold) and release determines then length of time the gain will take to return to normal once the signal level has dropped back below the threshold. You'll usually try to find the shortest release setting that doesn't result in obvious 'pumping', and the correct setting for most pop music applications is around a quarter of a second. The attack time should be fixed to its fastest setting to acquire tight control of vocals, but a slightly longer attack time allows the leading edge of transient sounds such as drums or guitars to cut through more strongly.

If a two-channel compressor is used on a whole stereo mix or stereo subgroup it's important that the unit has a Stereo Link switch. Without this the loudest channel will receive the most compression, which can cause the stereo image to shift from side to side.

Limiting

A limiter is basically a compressor with a very high ratio and a quick response time. Limiting is a vitally important function in PA work because it's very often only the limiter that stands between the drivers and a smoky death! If a general-purpose compressor is used as a limiter it must be set to its fastest attack time, but using a dedicated limiter is a better option if you don't already have them built into your crossovers or system processors.

Gates And Expanders

A gate is little more than an automatic switch which turns off the audio signal path when the signal falls below a threshold set by the user to mute low-level noise during pauses. Like compressors, most commercial gates have attack and release parameters that determine how quickly the gate opens and closes.

The fastest attack settings allow percussive transient sounds to pass through cleanly, while a slow attack forces the gate to open more gradually. Unwanted clicking can be avoided when gating non-percussive sounds by slowing the gate's attack time down to a few milliseconds. Percussive sounds usually require the fastest attack time possible in order to maintain their transient impact.

A variable release time means that the gate can close gradually when sounds with a slow decay are being processed. If the gate were to close abruptly the tail ends of naturally decaying sounds, such as reverb tails or decaying plucked guitars, would be cut off. Figure 4.3 shows the attack and release phases of a typical gate.

Side-Chain Filtering

An example of a more elaborate gating process is side-chain filtering, which usually comprises a pair of shelving equalisers – one high pass and one low pass – connected in series with the gate's side chain. By adjusting the upper and lower limits of the filters it's possible to make the gate open only when it 'hears' the band of frequencies between the two filter settings. This can help enormously in situations where spill from other instruments is likely to cause false triggering.

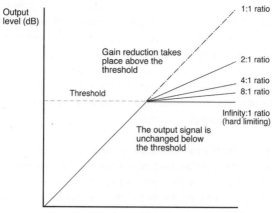

Figure 4.3: Graph of compressor action

Filtering is often used when miking drum kits in order to prevent crash cymbals from opening tom gates, and this is achieved by lowering the upper filter frequency to exclude the high frequencies of the cymbals but still allow the sound of the tom to trigger the gate.

Exciters And Enhancers

An equaliser can only affect frequencies that are already present, whereas an enhancer can actually create new high frequencies to provide the illusion that the sound is actually clearer and brighter than it originally was. Most exciters or enhancers combine elements of dynamic equalisation with other processes, including harmonic synthesis and phase manipulation. Not all manufacturers use the same combination of principles, and the outcome of this is that each type of enhancer has its own characteristic sound. However, most models produce a sense of increased clarity and projection.

Over-enhancing a signal can produce a harsh, fatiguing result that sounds particularly bad through PA horns. Enhancers are useful tools, but they must be used with restraint. Even so, they're valuable tools for projecting the vocals in difficult situations.

Connections

Gates, expander, limiters, compressors, equalisers and enhancers all fall under the umbrella of processors, and so should always be connected in line with a signal, usually via the mixing console's channel or group insert points. They will not work in the aux send/return system in the same way as effects, such as reverb or delay. You should also be aware that, on many pieces of balanced equipment, the practise of patching balanced-to-unbalanced leads into insert points which are unbalanced can result in a loss in level of 6dB.

Effects invariably involve some form of delay circuitry, and examples include reverb, delay, echo, chorus, flanging, vibrato and pitch shift. Not all of these effects require the original signal to be mixed with the treated signal, but all of them use delays, even if these are very short.

Effects such as those mentioned later in this chapter may be connected either via the (post-fade) aux send/return system or they may be used at the console insert points. When used in the aux send system the dry signal level should be turned off at the effects unit, but when used via insert points the dry/effect balance must be set on the effects unit itself.

Effects

Effects were once confined to tape echo, spring reverb and guitar amp tremolo, but these days, if it can be done in the studio, it can be done on stage. There are a number of cheap multi-effects units available that can generate anything from rotary-speaker simulations and chorus effects to delay and reverb, often in quite complex combinations.

Digital Delay

Digital delay is the successor to the tape echo unit, a special type of recorder which used one record head

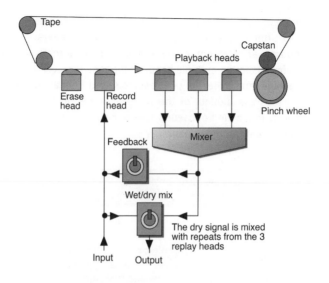

Figure 4.4: Operation of a tape-echo unit

and between one and four replay heads. A DDL (Digital Delay Line) is one of the key elements of a modern multi-effects unit, performing essentially the same task as the tape-loop echo machine, but it has no tapes to wear out and its range of adjustment is greater by an order of magnitude. It's also possible to modulate the delay time to create effects such as chorus, vibrato, flanging and phasing. Some models also offer multitap delay, which can create several repeats at different delay times. This is directly analogous to the multiple heads of the tape-loop echo machine, and by feeding back some signal from all of the taps the density of the repeats builds up very quickly into a kind of pseudo reverb. Figure 4.5 shows how a multitap delay operates.

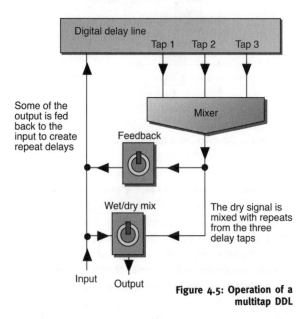

Figure 4.5: Operation of a multitap DDL

Delay Effects

The DDL is the basic component of a number of familiar effects, some of which are produced by modulating the delay time. The simplest DDL effect, however, is a single repeat which uses no modulation and no feedback. Short delays of between 30ms and 100ms are used to create slap-back echoes, while longer delays produce a distinct single echo. Also, delays timed to coincide with the tempo of the song can occasionally be effective.

Multiple equally-spaced delays can be obtained by increasing the feedback value, while using a multi-tapped delay enables a less rhythmic echo effect to be created. For the best effect, however, the delay times of the various tapes should not be set to exact multiples of each other. This simulates the multihead tape echo system, on which the heads were often spaced at irregular intervals. The addition of feedback causes the echo decay to become quite complex, and this effect is popularly used with electric guitars, vocals and instruments such as lead synths, saxophones and flutes.

A number of modern units feature a tap tempo facility, by which you simply tap your foot on a switch at the tempo of the song and the delay time will be set to the time interval between your taps. Obviously the maximum delay time can't exceed the maximum delay time of your DDL, but this is a very quick and easy way of making sure your that repeats are in time with the song.

Delay Modulation

Modulating the delay time with an LFO causes the pitch of the delayed signal to waver both sharp and flat at the rate set by the speed of the LFO. The depth of modulation determines the extent of the sound's sharpness or flatness. The simplest modulation effect is pitch vibrato, which only uses the delayed sound – the original sound is turned off by using the mix parameter. The sound emitted by the output will be delayed slightly, but if the delay time is set to less than 10ms it will be too short to notice.

Phasing

To convert vibrato into phasing, you should set the mix parameter to provide equal amounts of dry and delayed sound and experiment with delay times between 1ms and 10ms. As you adjust the speed and depth of modulation you'll hear the individual harmonics that make up the sound moving in and out of phase with each other, which has the effect of filtering the sound in a very dynamic and complex way. You'll probably recognise the effect as being similar to that obtained with guitar phaser pedals. Try switching on your unit's feedback invert function, if it has one, as this also affects the harmonic structure of the effect.

Flanging

Flanging dates back to the Sixties, and was first created by simultaneously running two tape machines carrying copies of the same music and then mixing the two outputs with precisely equal levels. If the two machines are perfectly in sync (synchronised) with each other then the two signals combine normally, but if the timing between the machines drifts the listener hears a phasing effect, caused by comb filtering. You can control the effect by deliberately slowing down first one machine and then the other by placing your hand on the supply reel.

Flanging can be approximated digitally by adding a delayed signal to the original sound and then modulating the delay time of the delayed signal. The settings for flanging are similar to those used for phasing but with longer delay times, typically 10-50ms, and the feedback value is increased to make the effect more resonant. As with phasing, inverting the phase of the signal fed back to the input allows different harmonics to be accentuated by filtering. Try both and decide which you prefer.

Chorus

Chorus is essentially the same as vibrato, although with an equal proportion of the dry sound mixed in. The idea of chorus is to produce the illusion of two instruments playing together by simulating the slight differences in timing and pitching that occur between two or more performers playing identical parts on identical instruments. By setting a longer delay time than for vibrato – for example, between 30ms and 150ms – the effect of the differences in timing between instruments becomes more pronounced. Chorus was first developed for use on electric guitars and synth string machines, but it can be used on virtually anything, from fretless bass to synth pads. You can also fatten up a mono chorus by panning the original, untreated sound to one side and the modulated delay to the other, which results in a wide, moving sound source that appears to hang between the speakers.

Algorithms

Modulation effects in a multi-effects unit are likely to have their own algorithms, making it unnecessary for the user to create the effect from scratch using a general-purpose DDL block. Irrelevant parameters will normally be excluded and the delay time range will be restricted to that relevant to the particular modulation effect being created. This helps to guide the inexperienced user in the right direction, and may provide the manufacturer with the opportunity to introduce further parameters to increase the flexibility of the effect.

Reverberation

Reverberation is a very familiar effect, and in nature it is created when sound reflects from surfaces inside a confined space, such as a building. Although the concept is simple the resulting reflection patterns are immensely complex, which is why electronic reverb processors require powered digital signal processing chips for their operation. Most reverb units include algorithms for halls, rooms, chambers and plates (a mechanical studio reverb device based on a large metal plate), as well as non-natural reverbs such as gated and reversed versions. Figure 4.6 illustrates how reverb develops from a percussive sound. The basic algorithms also include parameters for adjusting the relative high-frequency and low-frequency decay times to emulate the effects of different types of room or soft furnishings.

Gated Reverb

Gated reverb was originally achieved by miking a drum kit in an extremely live room and then using a noise gate to abruptly cut off the reverb at the end of each beat. Although this effect is less fashionable and is

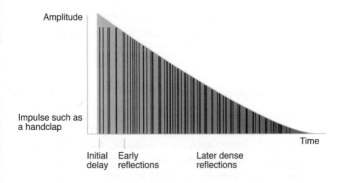

rarely used in this situation today, most multi-effects devices and reverb boxes are equipped with an option for gated reverb. This is sometimes a single algorithm, while on other units you may have to create it from separate reverb and gate 'blocks'. Reverse reverb is very similar, and comprises a burst of early reflections starting off at a low level and gradually increasing before ending abruptly. This reverse envelope is responsible for the reversed illusion created by the effect.

Pitch Shifting

Pitch shifting is a process which changes the pitch of a sound without changing its duration, an effect unlike that obtained from simply speeding up a tape machine. The range available to a pitch shifter is usually one or two octaves up or down, along with fine tuning and semitone step adjustment.

Most multi-effects devices are fitted with a pitch shifting section, which may allow you to simultaneously shift material up and down in pitch. If small shifts of between five and ten cents (hundredths of a semitone) are applied to a signal, both positive and negative, this can provide an effective alternative to chorusing without the risk of running into any obvious cyclic sweeping.

Multi-Effects Units

There are now numerous multi-effects boxes on the market, most of which provide the ability to apply reverb, delay, modulated delay, pitch shifting and equalisation to your music, while some may also offer compression, gating and specialist effects such as vocoding and the emulation of rotary speakers. Simpler multi-effects units may be limited in that they are only able to connect the individual effect blocks in a series chain, and the simplest of these units place the blocks in a preset order, which then leaves the user with little choice other than that of which blocks to use and which of them to turn off. More sophisticated systems allow the user to rearrange the blocks into a different order, and it's quite common for both series and parallel connection to be permitted. Figure 4.7 shows both series and parallel routing options.

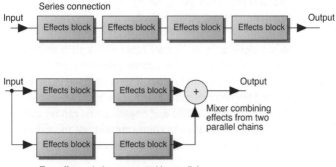

Figure 4.7: Series and parallel routing options

Amp/Speaker Simulators

The loudspeakers and enclosures used in guitar and bass amplification tend to have a very limited frequency response, which enables them to filter out the rougher-sounding components of amplifier distortion. Speaker simulation is often included as part of a multi-effects box's repertoire, which means that, for very small gigs or solo performances with backing tapes, guitar players are able to plug their effects box directly into the PA system and play through that rather than having to take a separate amplifier with them.

Anti-Feedback Systems

Acoustic feedback is the enemy of every live performer, and the most popular manner of controlling it is by using a graphic equaliser to 'notch out' those troublesome frequencies at which it occurs. Once your system is set up, the geometry and acoustic properties of the room, combined with the characteristics of your sound system, will cause feedback to occur at some frequencies before it does at others. During the setup procedure, using conventional graphic equalisers, the system gain is increased until the ringing that announces the onset of feedback appears, and the appropriate graphic slider is then pulled down slightly to restore stability. This 'ringing out' procedure is repeated for those frequencies at which the most serious feedback occurs, and in the hands of an experienced engineer the stability of a system can be increased significantly. However, this solution is far from perfect, and it can take even a skilled operator a considerable length of time to ring out a system.

Auto Anti-Feedback Devices

During the mid-Nineties, a new generation of processor was developed which was designed to simplify the control of feedback while at the same time having less of an audible effect on the sound coming from the PA. These processors, based on equalisers with very narrow frequency bands, automatically lock onto those frequencies at which feedback is detected during the ringing-out stage of the soundcheck.

Once the system gain has been increased to the point at which ringing occurs, the ring frequency is measured automatically and a very narrow notch filter is then positioned at that frequency to kill it. If the gain is increased even further, this will cause the system to ring at a new frequency, and a second filter will then move in to kill this ring. This process is then repeated until a number of filters are set in place, a situation which should suppress the strongest feedback modes.

Having worked with a number of anti-feedback devices which operate on the principle of filter tracking, I have to admit that they work surprisingly well, although the exact amount of extra gain which you can apply before feedback kicks in depends on the room you're in and on the quality of the other components in your system. Under typical circumstances it isn't unreasonable to expect an additional 5dB or 6dB of feedback-free gain, and as a bonus you'll probably find that your system will sound a lot clearer when it isn't ringing on the verge of feedback.

5 STAGE MIKING

At smaller gigs it may not be necessary to mic up the entire back line, but at larger venues it's important to know which mics to use and where to position them. This chapter explains why certain types of microphone are favoured for certain jobs and offers guidelines on positioning them.

Vocals

Vocal miking is relatively straightforward, as the usual aim is to position a dynamic cardioid as close to the singer as possible. Use a model specifically designed for vocals, as this will have a presence peak in the frequency response to help the singer's voice cut through. A good-quality mic stand is important, and it's a good idea to tape the mic cable to the stand, leaving a loop at the mic end, thus killing any vibrations coming along the cable. Although pop shields are always used in the studio there's no room for these in a live situation, and foam shields help little. For this reason, popping must be controlled by the singer – backing off slightly and singing over or under the mic is one way of controlling plosive 'B' and 'P' sounds, as well as keeping high-level phrases or words under control.

Electric Guitars

The miked sound from a guitar amp changes considerably depending on the position of the mic relative to the speaker. In a live situation the mic must be as near as possible to the speaker grille in order to exclude any spill, and you'll find that the brightest sound occurs when the mic is pointing directly towards the centre of the speaker cone. If you move the mic towards the edge of the cone, or if you angle it, the sound tends to become more mellow. Dynamic mics are generally best for guitar work, though certain players prefer the extra top end available with a capacitor microphone.

Microphone Positioning

You will sometimes see a mic hanging down by its lead in front of the guitar amp, but this is not usually the best way of using a cardioid mic as its most sensitive axis will be pointing directly at the floor. There'll probably be plenty of level, even so, but the off-axis sound of a mic is different to its on-axis sound (it's usually duller), so unless you've hit on a lucky combination that just happens to sound brilliant it's better to put the mic on a short stand and point it directly at the speaker, as shown in Figure 5.1. However, you should be aware that stage vibrations can enter the mic via the stand, so it may be prudent to switch in the low cut filter on the mixing desk. If there's more than one speaker in a cabinet, try to determine if one is better sounding than the others and then always mic that one. If the miked sound is too bright you can match the out-front sound to your

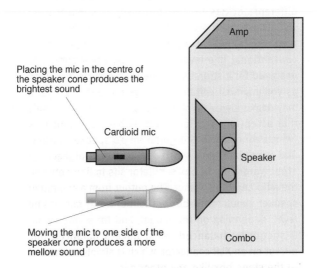

Placing the mic in the centre of the speaker cone produces the brightest sound

Cardioid mic

Amp

Speaker

Moving the mic to one side of the speaker cone produces a more mellow sound

Combo

Figure 5.1: Miking a guitar combo

on-stage sound more closely by moving the microphone away from the centre of the speaker cone slightly, rather than using the desk EQ from the outset. Once you've found the best match you can then use EQ to fine tune it.

Speaker Simulators

Most speaker simulators designed for live use can be fed either from a pre-amp output jack or from the loudspeaker outlet of the amp, but they usually provide different sockets for this purpose, as speaker-level signals are much bigger than line-level signals. Never feed the speaker output of an amplifier into a conventional line-level DI box or speaker simulator designed for instrument or line-level signals, however, as you'll almost certainly damage the DI box and you may damage your amplifier along with it. Most models that accept speaker-level signals have an input jack (which connects to the guitar amp's speaker output) and a thru jack, into which the speaker is plugged. In other words, the DI box/simulator sits in line between the amp and the speaker. The output from a combined speaker simulator/DI box will either be at mic or line level, depending on the model, and for serious work it should be balanced. Most have a balanced mic output on an XLR connector, which is simply connected to the stage box like any other mic.

Useful EQ Frequencies For Electric Guitars

- Boost at 120Hz to add punch to the sound of rock guitars.

- Cut below 100Hz or switch in the high-pass (low cut) filter to reduce low-frequency spill and stage vibration.

- Boost at 2-3kHz to add bite.

- Boost at 5-7kHz to add 'zing' to clean rhythm sounds.

- Cut at 200-300Hz if the sound seems boxy.

- Cut at above 5kHz to reduce edginess.

Bass Guitars

At one time pretty much everything was miked up, including the bass guitar and the keyboard amps. These days, however, bass is more likely to be DI'd, although miking is still an option preferred by some people. Part of this change is due to the evolution in styles of playing the bass, with cleaner sounds becoming more popular. There are excellent bass effects pre-amps available for those who want to have a DI'd sound to be like that of a real amp, along with effects. Bass guitars fitted with conventional non-active pickups must be used with a DI box between the bass guitar and the amplifier so that a low-impedance balanced feed can be fed to the mixer via the stage multicore. Active basses and guitars can be plugged directly into a desk, though it may still be beneficial to use a DI box in order to provide ground lifting as an insurance against hum.

Miking The Bass

If you prefer to mic up a bass amplification system, the procedure is similar to that used for regular guitar amplifiers. The main difference is that the mic is usually set up a few inches from the speaker grill rather than pressed right up against it. It's also useful to choose a mic that has a good bass response rather than a general-purpose mic on which the bass has been rolled off to prevent the proximity effect from making vocals sound too bass heavy. Modern bass styles also benefit from compression because the different techniques of plucking, slapping and pulling produce notes with wildly differing volume levels.

Chorus treatments work well on fretless basses, but they can also be used to good effect on conventional fretted basses, as long as they're used in moderation. Flanging is also a viable option, but because it's such an obvious effect it should be used sparingly.

Drums

A good drum sound starts with a good-sounding drum kit, and as long as it's fitted with heads that are in decent condition it should be possible to coax any reasonable kit into sounding halfway decent fairly quickly. On the other hand, a kit with worn heads and stretched snares is unlikely to sound great no matter what you do with it.

The simplest way to obtain a natural drum sound is to use a stereo microphone pair, usually spaced a few feet apart and positioned a few feet in front of the kit. This technique works well for styles such as jazz, where a natural acoustic kit sound is needed. For pop work, however, you should use additional close mics on the kick drum and snare to beef up the sound.

The snare mic (usually a dynamic cardioid) should be placed a couple of inches above and from the edge of the top head. The kick drum should also be miked with a dynamic cardioid microphone, ideally one with an extended bass response specifically designed for use with bass drums. This should be positioned inside the drum shell, pointing towards the spot hit by the beater. Most kick drums used for pop work have a hole cut in the front head, and a boom stand can be used to suspend the mic through this hole. If you don't have a suitable stand, you can obtain generally acceptable results simply by resting the mic on the damping blanket.

If you need to mic the toms as well, the usual position for mics in this case is a couple of inches above the drum head, a couple of inches in from the edge and angled towards the centre of the head, and any damping materials should be placed out of the way of the mic. This setup is more or less the same as the setup for the snare drum. If you're going to close mic all of the drums in this way it's best to bring the front stereo mics closer to the kit and position them above the drums so that they can pick up the ambience of the whole kit, as well as the cymbals. Figure 5.2 shows a fully-miked drum kit, although some of the stands have been omitted in the interests of clarity. If a separate hi-hat mic is necessary, capacitor or back-electret mics are best in this role because of their ability to handle high-frequency sounds. In most cases, however, you'll find that you're picking up enough hi-hat sound without needing to use a separate mic.

Damping Drums

If damping is needed, this is usually achieved by taping folded tissue or cloth to the edge of the top head of the drum, but be careful not to damp the drums too much or they'll sound lifeless when the other members

Figure 5.2: Close-miking the entire kit (with overheads)

Stereo overheads on tall booms positioned between two and five feet above the cymbals. These should ideally be capacitor microphones or back-electret models

Snare and tom mics positioned around two inches from the head and around two inches from the edge of the drum

Hi-hat mic is a capacitor model placed just above the top cymbal and a few inches to one side

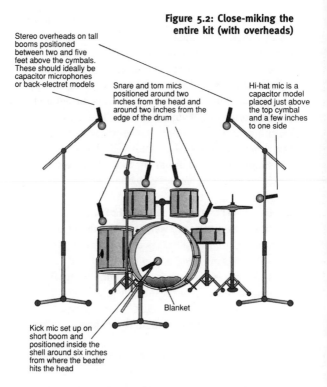

Blanket

Kick mic set up on short boom and positioned inside the shell around six inches from where the beater hits the head

of the band are playing. It's easy to get paranoid about rings and rattles, but most noises will be inaudible during the actual performance.

To damp the kick drum just place a folded woollen blanket inside the shell, and to increase the level of damping push the blanket so that it's in contact with more of the rear head. Noise gates are useful in tightening up bass drum sounds, as a surprising amount of spill from the snare drum and toms is picked up by the bass drum mic. If you have enough gates, it's often worth using them to clean up the toms, and if you're using them in this way then gates with side-chain filters are the easiest to set up, as the filters help to prevent any false triggering from the cymbals.

Useful Drum EQ Frequencies

- Boost at 80Hz to add weight to kick drums and low toms.

- Boost at 120-150Hz to add punch to toms and snares.

- Boost at 6kHz to add sizzle to cymbals.

- Boost at 2-3kHz to add definition to a snare drum.

- Cut at 150-250Hz to reduce boxiness.

- Cut at 1kHz to reduce harshness.

6 MONITORING

A stage monitoring system is essentially a second PA system with the speakers directed back at the performers, and the complexity of these systems can vary enormously. At its simplest everyone might hear the same monitor mix, while a more complex monitoring system might involve a dedicated monitor console capable providing each performer with their ideal mix. Unfortunately, using foldback can increase the risk of experiencing feedback. For example, the electric guitar, bass and keyboard can all be amplified to any practical level to balance the drums, but there is a limit to how much amplification can be applied to vocals before feedback becomes a problem. Also, because miked drums sound quite different to an acoustic kit, they are usually routed through the PA system for all but the smallest gigs.

Without monitoring vocalists are at a particular disadvantage, as they will experience great difficulty in hearing their own voices above the several hundreds of watts of backline amplification being churned out only feet away. And as any singer knows, if you can't hear yourself sing it's virtually impossible to keep perfectly in tune. This was the situation at the end of the Sixties, when bands were playing at relatively large venues, and even stadia, with no foldback monitoring.

The Floor Wedge

The most familiar model of stage monitor is the floor wedge, which is a triangular speaker cabinet that sits at the feet of the performer and directs a foldback mix towards their position. Wedge monitors are generally two-way speaker systems comprising either a twelve-inch speaker or a 15-inch speaker with a horn driver handling the top end, although there are smaller systems that are available for bands playing smaller venues. These wedges often include passive crossover systems, though it's also possible to buy active monitors equipped with integral power amplifiers and crossovers.

In small to medium-sized PA systems, stage monitors are driven from the pre-fade foldback sends of the main mixing console, although larger touring systems are equipped with the added sophistication of a separate monitor console, usually operated from the side of the stage. Figure 6.1 shows a system where two different monitor mixes are fed to two pairs of floor wedges via a two-channel power amplifier.

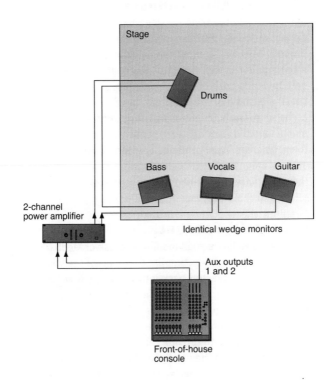

Figure 6.1: A typical monitor system

Monitors And Feedback

Setting up loudspeakers on stage might seem like the perfect recipe for feedback, and if things aren't done properly then this is most certainly the case. However, if the monitor is well designed, has a good dispersion pattern and is positioned in the blind spot of a cardioid vocal mic, some of the vocal mix can be directed back at the singer without increasing the risk of feedback too much. Cardioid mics are least sensitive directly behind them, whereas hyper-cardioids are least sensitive at an angle of around 45° from their rear axis. Figure 6.2 shows the polar patterns of cardioid and hypercardioid mics in relation to their ideal monitor positions.

Causes Of Feedback

Even with a well-designed monitor, the risk of feedback is increased because an amplified version of the vocal signal is being directed back into the general vicinity of the microphone. Feedback will always start to build up at just one frequency when the various parameters of directivity, room resonance and system frequency response conspire to provide the most gain. If any EQ boost is applied to the vocal then the boosted section of the audio band is especially vulnerable to feedback.

This situation can be improved by using either a graphic or parametric equaliser in the monitor feed to apply

Cardioid. The least sensitive area is directly behind the mic, so it helps to tilt the mic at around 45° in order to minimise monitor spill. The monitor should be directly behind the mic

Hypercardioid. The least sensitive area is around 45 degrees away from the rear axis of the mic, so it may be best to keep the mic level and to offset the monitor to one side by around 45°. Check your mic spec sheet to find the exact position of the deaf spot

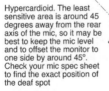

Figure 6.2: Mic and monitor positions

cut in the frequency bands which are causing problems, although this procedure relies on the expertise of the user for its success. Some graphic equalisers are now available with LEDs above the sliders, which helps to pinpoint troublesome feedback frequencies and makes setting up a lot easier. However, it's important not to try too hard when notching out all the feedback frequencies if you're using a graphic EQ because you'll probably find that you've also notched out most of what you wanted to hear in the first place! The problem is that even a 30-band graphic equaliser affects almost an octave when a single fader is moved, yet the feedback frequency which you're trying to combat may be less than $1/_{20}$ of an octave wide. If you are using a graphic equaliser it's probably best to ring out by increasing the system gain gradually until ringing starts and then cutting only the worst offending bands by just a few decibels.

Monitor systems may feed back at different frequencies to the main PA because of the locations of the speakers, so it's useful to have separate equalisers for the main PA and the monitor system. On larger PA rigs there may be a separate graphic equaliser for each monitor speaker, but each will be individually set up by ringing-out the system as just described.

Feedback Eliminators

In recent years a number of companies have developed dedicated feedback suppressors which automatically identify the frequencies that are causing trouble and then apply appropriate filtering at those frequencies.

These devices have two main advantages over simple graphic equalisers: firstly, they set themselves up automatically, which means that the engineer doesn't need to be very experienced; and secondly, the filters used in these devices are usually much narrower than those used in conventional graphic equalisers, which means that more cut can be applied in a greater number of bands without the overall PA or monitor sound being significantly affected. Setting them up is much like ringing out a PA system, with the exception that, as the gain is increased, the filters automatically lock onto and remove the feedback frequencies as they crop up. Most systems provide a set number of filters that lock onto feedback during the ringing out procedure, but additional filters are provided to tackle any feedback that may arise during the performance because a singer moves a microphone. Consult the chapter on 'Effects And Processors' for more details on these devices.

Monitor Positioning

Perhaps the most important factor to consider when using monitors (other than their quality) is their position, especially when working in small venues, where the stage area may not be exactly conventional. Indeed, many pub venues are so cramped that there may be insufficient room for floor monitors to work properly at all, in which case it can be more effective to use just a pair of monitors or a spare pair of small PA cabinets to provide coverage for the whole band. These can be placed on top of or just behind the main PA speakers, pointing backwards at the opposite corner of the stage area. This catches the whole band in the crossfire, and because their distance from the monitors is greater than usual the sound is dispersed more effectively before it is reflected. This setup, shown in Figure 6.3, operates on almost the same principle as side-fill monitors in a large PA rig, albeit on a smaller scale.

In smaller pub and club venues it may be adequate to use one pair of monitors positioned behind the main PA speakers and angled so that they converge on the position occupied by the vocal mic or mics

Vocal mic

Monitor speaker set up as cross fill

Main PA speaker

Figure 6.3: Monitors positioned behind PA speakers

Monitor Spill

In a larger PA setup, where the entire band – rather than just the vocalist – has monitors, the setting-up procedure becomes a little more complex, because not only must the vocal monitors be positioned to avoid feedback but everybody else's monitors also have to be arranged so that they don't spill too much sound into the vocal mic. If this isn't achieved, the overall vocal sound through the PA will be seriously compromised and the engineer will have less chance of setting up a workable balance. In such a system it's more likely that each monitor will have its own power amplifier and will be fed from a different pre-fade (foldback) send, enabling each performer to hear a different mix. The best way to minimise spill, however, is to position each monitor as close to the person using it as possible, so that it will require less overall level. It's important that the monitors are angled correctly so that the sound is directed towards a performer's head, not his or her knees!

Another practical approach is to use a much smaller monitor – still designed for good dispersion – and mount it on a mic stand very close to the person using it. These monitors are similar to miniature hi-fi speakers but with higher power-handling capabilities, and generally come with moulded plastic cases. Many of the larger companies which manufacture PAs make compact installation speakers that would do the job very well, and there are mic stand fittings available for many of these speakers.

In-Ear Monitors

In-ear monitoring is one of the more recent developments in PA technology, but the principle is very simple. Instead of using on-stage loudspeakers to provide the monitoring signal, each performer wears a pair of in-ear phones similar to those used with high-quality personal hi-fi systems. These require only a small amount of amplifier power, and singers who move around the stage can take their monitoring with them rather than wandering out of range of a floor wedge. All of the commercial systems I've tried come with a radio transmitter and receiver exactly like those used for radio microphones, but in reverse. Both VHF and UHF systems may be used, depending on available budget and the requirements of the venue. VHF systems are more prone to interference than UHF systems but are also cheaper.

On their own, most in-ear headphones allow too much sound to leak into the ear from backline amplification and other sources, so the better systems involve custom ear moulds, where each headphone is fixed to a soft rubber earplug moulded from the user's own ear canal.

These are fairly expensive to make but they're infinitely better than struggling with off-the-shelf headphones. The better models include an adjustable vent which allows the performer to choose exactly how much spill to allow in from the outside world.

By excluding a large proportion of the spill the performer can monitor at a lower (and less potentially damaging) level, and a limiter is included in most professional systems to prevent the monitoring from exceeding safe levels. As you might expect, the bass response of these devices is a little limited so they won't satisfy the drummer who insists on 2kW of side fills, but in all other respects the concept is a good one, and I'm sure it will become more widely used in the near future.

Overview

Some form of monitoring is desirable even in very small venues, but trying to use large wedge monitors in a tiny pub can be disastrous. The type of monitor you use should be properly designed, with even dispersion characteristics, or it will simply provoke feedback. Even a well-designed monitor must be used carefully and positioned where it's least likely to cause trouble.

Using two wedge monitors or compact PA cabs as side fills is often enough if you don't want to buy a lot of

extra monitoring equipment, and if small speakers on
stands don't intrude too much visually then stand-
mounted mini monitors are very useful for performers
who don't need to move around too much. In-ear
systems also have a lot going for them, but the initial
investment when using these is quite high as it includes
the radio links and limiters. What's more, while some
performers love working with them, some can't get used
to them at all.

7 PRACTICALITIES

Assuming that you can play and you've rehearsed your songs, obtaining the best possible sound on stage can only happen if you choose the right equipment on both the back line and the PA. Backline arrangements are largely a matter of individual taste, but if it needs help from the PA you'll need to ensure that this is powerful enough to deal with the extra work – particularly the drums and bass guitar. This requirement has to be balanced against the available transporting space and budget. Perfectly acceptable results can be achieved with a fairly compact system (as long as it's used within its design limitations), but to handle bass frequencies effectively you'll need separate bass or sub-bass cabinets.

Amplifier Power

A rock band with a drum kit is obviously going to need a more powerful system than a folk band. If you're performing small pub gigs, with the PA handling mainly vocals, then a system of just a few hundred watts per channel, driven from a powered mixer, is a practical choice. In most pub venues it's more of a problem to get the drums quiet enough than it is to get them loud enough. On the other hand, if you want to amplify everything, a couple of kilowatts is probably the minimum possible amount that you can apply, given that an acoustic drum kit can emit as much power as a 400W amplifier on its own. If you feel that your existing amplification is being pushed to its limit most of the time, fitting a dedicated limiter before the power amp will prevent the peaks from clipping. This will enable you to achieve a noticeably higher average power level without running the risk of feeding distorted signals to your drivers.

Whatever PA system you choose, it's vital that the loudspeakers have reasonably flat frequency responses, especially stage monitors used near vocal mics. Any significant humps or spikes in their frequency responses will increase the risk of feedback, and will also compromise the sound.

Coverage Characteristics

Speakers must also have properly controlled dispersion characteristics. Unless a system is carefully designed, it's easy to end up with a system which has a very wide dispersion at low frequencies and a relatively narrow dispersion at higher frequencies. As a consequence, although the high frequencies might make it to the back of the room, they will tend to sound rather honky, and listeners off axis from the speakers will receive inadequate coverage.

Small-System Benefits

In smaller venues the performance of full-range cabinets is more predictable, they're easy to transport, and they're also a lot easier to set up, especially if they're small enough to be put on tripod stands. Because full-range cabinets can be designed and built to use matched acoustic components, the performance of a system comprising these is likely to be more accurate than one comprising bass, mid-range and horn cabinets from different sources. There's also less risk of making wrong connections.

A typical full-range PA cab with an integral passive crossover requires just a single twin-core speaker cable between it and the amplifier. Active systems are usually fed from an amp rack via a multiway cable terminating in a multipin connector at the cabinet end, though for the ultimate in convenience it makes sense to use the new generation of moulded plastic full-range enclosures with integral power amps and active crossovers.

Bass Handling

Even a relatively compact system with a fairly flat

frequency response can give adequately controlled directivity over the entire audio spectrum if it's properly designed. The main compromise that must be made with portable, full-range cabinets is in their capacity for handling bass, so for gigs where you're going to be relying on them to reinforce the drums and bass you can use additional sub-bass speakers driven from separate power amplifiers. These are run from a crossover, which removes all of the low bass energy from the main speakers and directs only low bass energy to the bass speakers. Some smaller systems achieve this by using passive crossovers, although systems which use an active crossover and an additional power amplifier for the bass cabinet generally produce better results. Not only does the addition of dedicated bass speakers improve the bass handling of the system but, by removing some of the low-frequency burden from the main PA cabinets, it also allows the entire system to be used at a higher level.

Powered-Mixer Benefits

Mixer amplifiers provide a convenient means of driving a small PA, and a number of more recent models also include digital reverb, which means that you don't have to buy an external processor, the amount of wiring required is reduced to a bare minimum, and the system can be set up very quickly. The obvious disadvantages are that, if there's a serious failure, you've lost both your power amps and your mixer, and that, if you want more power than is available, you'll have to buy external power amplifiers, thus cancelling out the advantage of compactness. However, it may be possible to switch the internal amplifiers to run your stage monitor system, in which case the addition of external power amplifiers to drive the main PA is a sensible upgrade path. If you're intending to add sub-bass speakers at some stage it's worth choosing a mixer amp equipped with a built-in active crossover (or the provision to fit one) to cater for that eventuality. However, powered mixers are limited in that longer speaker cables must be used, as they have to run all the way from the mixer to the speakers.

Setting Up A PA System

Sound levels diminish as you move further from the source, so it stands to reason that the further away your mics are positioned from the speakers the more level you can use before feedback becomes a problem. Because PA speakers are directional devices they should be positioned in front of the mics, facing away from the performers. Even if you have to compromise on the position of the PA because of the room layout, you should still try to get the backs of the PA speakers facing towards your stage mics.

basic Live Sound

People are better at absorbing sound than reflecting it or transmitting it, so it's pretty obvious that, if the people at the back are going to be able to hear properly, the speakers need to be angled above the heads of the audience in the front rows. Separate speakers can be used in a large concert system to cover different sections of the audience, but in smaller venues the same speakers are heard by front and back rows alike. Unfortunately, simply standing the speaker cabinets on tables or erecting them on stands that can't be tilted isn't always the ideal solution, as Figure 7.1 illustrates.

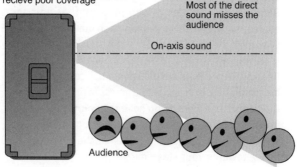

Most of the on-axis sound is directed over the audience's heads and reflects from the rear wall of the venue. Also, the front rows of the audience recieve poor coverage

Most of the direct sound misses the audience

On-axis sound

Audience

Figure 7.1: Speakers in a level position

The problem here is that the on-axis sound passes over the heads of all the audience until it hits the rear wall of the venue, whereupon it is reflected back into the room. This means that the audience will hear less level in the first place and the reflections from the back wall will interfere with the direct sound, making it reverberant and unclear. It also means that more sound energy will be reflected back to the stage, where there's a greater chance of your mics picking it up, causing the system to feed back.

Angled Cabinets

A better solution is to position the cabinets a little higher and angle them downwards so that they're aimed at a spot around two thirds of the way towards the back of the audience, an arrangement illustrated in Figure 7.2. If you have speaker cabinets that use 'top hat' adaptors to fix them on top of tripod stands, the chances are that they won't be able to be tilted. A DIY solution to this problem is to fit a second top-hat adaptor to the speaker cabinet at an angle, as shown in Figure 7.3.

By angling the speaker cabinets down slightly, the on-axis sound is directed towards the back of the audience, which helps to compensate for the fact that the people are further away. At the same time, those at the front

basic Live Sound

If the speakers are angled towards
the rear of the audience, less sound
reaches the rear wall and the front
rows of the audience receive better
coverage

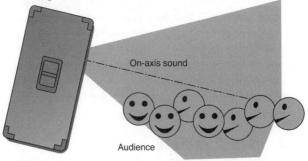

Figure 7.2: Speakers tilted downwards

of the venue won't be deafened because they're hearing
the lower-level off-axis sound. Listeners nearer the front
are more off axis, but as they are proportionally nearer
the speakers the actual sound level they hear is
comparable to what's heard at the back.

Wall Reflections

Position your speakers carefully to minimise unwanted
reflections from walls or the ceiling. In an ideal situation
all of the front-of-house sound would be directed at
your audience and none at the walls or ceilings, and

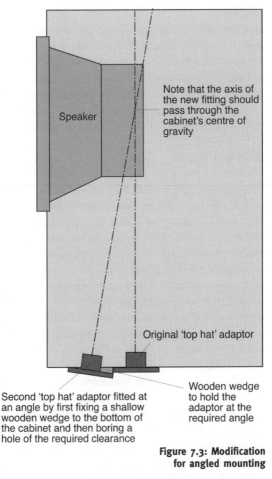

Note that the axis of the new fitting should pass through the cabinet's centre of gravity

Speaker

Original 'top hat' adaptor

Second 'top hat' adaptor fitted at an angle by first fixing a shallow wooden wedge to the bottom of the cabinet and then boring a hole of the required clearance

Wooden wedge to hold the adaptor at the required angle

Figure 7.3: Modification for angled mounting

even though this isn't possible in practice you should still aim to get as close to this ideal as you can. Reflected sound can never be completely eliminated, but you should worry most about those walls closest to the speakers, so try to angle the speakers in such a way that the reflections travel away from you and don't end up bouncing back onto the stage.

More Power

There may come a time when you need to double up your speakers and amplifiers to provide you with more power for larger venues. You might imagine that to double the level of your system all you'd need to do is add another power amp, along with two more cabinets placed alongside the original pair. However, this isn't necessarily the most practical solution. For the sake of argument, let's say that these speakers have their -6dB point (the point at which the measured SPL is exactly half of what it was when measured on axis) at 15º off axis. If you visualise the sound coming out of the speakers in beams, as shown in Figure 7.4, these beams will overlap, causing an accumulation of power along an axis between the two enclosures, although there will also be both phase additions and cancellations at various frequencies in the off-axis sound. The result is that the useful angle of dispersion of the cabinets is narrowed if they are standing side by side.

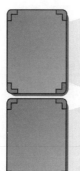

Mounting speakers side by side causes the patterns to overlap, which can lead to coloration of off-axis sounds

Top view of speakers

Figure 7.4: Cabinets arranged side by side reduce horizontal dispersion

A better way to use two speaker cabinets together is to stand them at an angle to each other, as shown in Figure 7.5. The angle between the cabinets should be twice the -6dB dispersion angle of the speakers, and in our previous example, where the -6dB point occurs at 15º, the required angle should be 30º. In this way the dispersion patterns of the speakers will overlap at -6dB, providing more even power coverage over a wider angle. The on-axis sound may be no louder than that

Figure 7.5: Cabinets angled for wider horizontal dispersion

Angling the speakers provides wider coverage and avoids unnecessary overlapping

Speakers
(top view)

coming from a single cabinet, but the angle of coverage will be wider, so you'll be able to pump more sound energy into the room. Alternatively, you can stand one cabinet on top of the other – a technique which will be described shortly.

What would be really useful is some way of controlling the dispersion of the PA speakers, but enclosures sadly don't come equipped with a dispersion control knob. However, if you're using two or more identical cabinets on each side, you can stack them in such a way that the desired result can be achieved, as shown in Figure 7.6. Here, the top cabinet has been inverted in order to align the two high-frequency drivers as close together as possible. This produces a narrowing of the vertical dispersion of the mid and high frequencies without significantly affecting dispersion in the horizontal plane.

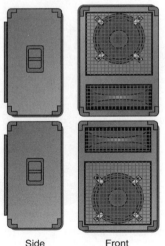

Inverting the top speaker will narrow the dispersion pattern in the vertical plane

Side   Front

Figure 7.6: Cabinets stacked to reduce vertical dispersion

Early Column Speakers

In the early days of band PA development, speakers were often built as vertical columns containing four drivers (often with no HF units at all), both to maintain a narrow visual profile and also because the tall, thin nature of a column produced good horizontal dispersion and relatively narrow vertical dispersion. In venues such as cinemas or theatres, which combine high ceilings with tiered seating, it may be desirable to increase the

Angling the top speaker will increase the dispersion angle in the vertical plane. Both speakers are the normal way up

Side   Front

Figure 7.7: Cabinets stacked with top enclosure angled

vertical dispersion of the PA, and the easiest way to do this is to stack the cabinets (this time the same way up) with the top one angled back slightly, as shown in Figure 7.7. As a rule of thumb, a good technique is to line up the top cabinet by eye so that it's directed somewhere towards the rear third of the audience.

Acoustic Feedback

Acoustic feedback is the number one enemy in small venues, and, as explained earlier, the likelihood of feedback arising is not directly related to the loudness of the system but instead to how much gain is being used. A singer with a loud voice performing close to a microphone is much less likely to encounter feedback problems than someone with a weak voice who doesn't keep close to the mic. There will always be some sound from the PA speakers that gets back into the vocal mics (even the pros can't prevent this entirely), but to keep it under control the system gain must be kept below the point at which feedback starts to build up.

Vocal Microphones

Good vocal mics are essential in any system because, like speakers, poor mics might have humps in their frequency responses which encourage feedback. Most vocal microphones have a deliberate presence peak at around 2-4kHz to help with clarity, but the rest of the response should be nominally flat, with a gentle roll off at the low end. A good cardioid or hypercardioid dynamic vocal mic is fine for most applications.

Hypercardioid mics have the most tightly-controlled pickup pattern, but they are more sensitive than cardioids to sounds coming from directly behind. For this reason the back of a hypercardioid mic shouldn't be aimed at a either stage monitor or a PA speaker. It's a better idea to aim it at something absorbent, such as the audience. Also, although it's important to choose a microphone that has good feedback rejection characteristics, it's also important to choose one that suits the singer's voice.

Microphone Technique

The loudest results are obtained when the singer's lips are almost touching the wire grille of the mic. It's also important that the vocalist sings directly into the end of the mic rather than across the top of it, as so many club entertainers seem to do, although singing slightly off axis can improve a particularly bad popping problem. Also, switching in the low cut filter on the mixing console can help reduce low-frequency booming and popping.

Figure 7.8 shows the correct mic position for a cardioid microphone. However, the proximity effect associated

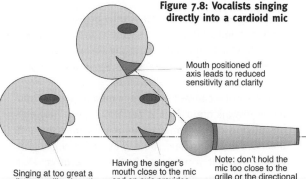

Figure 7.8: Vocalists singing directly into a cardioid mic

Mouth positioned off axis leads to reduced sensitivity and clarity

Singing at too great a distance will reduce the mic's sensitivity and may allow unwanted sounds to overpower the vocals

Having the singer's mouth close to the mic and on axis provides the most sensitivity. The proximity effect will increase the bass warmth of the sound

Note: don't hold the mic too close to the grille or the directional characteristics will suffer, increasing the risk of acoustic feedback

with cardioid and hypercardioid mics causes a noticeable bass boost whenever the mic is used very close to the lips, and although experienced performers can vary their distance from the microphone to make deliberate tonal changes, inexperienced singers may end up producing an uneven sound. A good way of practising mic technique is to set up some headphones at home so that you can hear tonal changes as you move the microphone away from your mouth.

It's very important to hold the microphone so that your hand isn't touching the wire basket or blocking any of the small vents which appear directly below the basket on some mics. These vents create the directional characteristic of the mic – covering them up prevents them from working and the mic is likely to feed back.

If you're using conventional stage monitoring and you prefer to walk around while performing, you may end up moving out of range of your own monitor and therefore unable to hear yourself as well as you'd like. What's more, if you move into the range of another musician's stage monitor you might cause feedback problems, unless you make sure that the mic's dead axis is kept pointing towards the monitor.

Spill

Next to feedback, spill is a major cause of live sound problems. Anything loud going on directly behind the singer will also be picked up and amplified, so it's sensible to try to position the vocalist as far away from backline amplification or drums as possible, and also to ensure that no backline is positioned directly behind the mic. A guitar amp on a low stand or chair won't cause as much trouble as a speaker stack positioned at microphone height if it's close to the mic.

Even if spill from the back line is minimised by careful positioning of the mic, there's still spill from the main

PA speakers to consider. At low frequencies you can't do much about this except use the low cut filters on all of your vocal mic channels. However, spill can also rebound from the rear wall of the stage and into your vocal mics, and the closer they are to the rear wall the more likely you'll run into feedback problems. In small or cramped venues you could consider hanging a heavy curtain behind the singer to absorb some of the sound.

Stage Monitors

Stage monitors are also a common source of feedback problems because they must be positioned close to the singers. They should ideally be positioned at around 45° to the rear of a hypercardioid mic or directly behind a cardioid mic, where the mics are least sensitive. This arrangement is shown in Figure 7.9.

Monitor EQ

To produce the maximum level possible before running into feedback you'll generally have to equalise your monitors to notch out troublesome frequencies with a graphic equaliser or automatic feedback reduction unit.

The EQ settings needed to tame feedback will vary from system to system and venue to venue because they depend on the PA speakers, the monitor speakers, the types of mics and the positions of all of these

Cardioid. The least sensitive area is directly behind the mic, so it helps to tilt the mic at around 45° in order to minimise monitor spill. The monitor should be directly behind the mic

Side view

Above view

Hypercardioid. The least sensitive area is around 45° away from the rear axis of the mic, so it may be best to keep the mic level and to offset the monitor to one side by around 45°

Figure 7.9: Monitor positions relative to a vocal mic

components within the room. The shape and size of the room also has a significant influence, as does the nature and position of the room's reflective surfaces.

If you're using graphic equalisers, you'll need to ring out the system during the soundcheck and then apply cut in those frequency bands where feedback is becoming a problem. The usual method of setting up your system to achieve this is to start off with all of the EQ faders flat, then increase the system gain during the soundcheck until feedback starts, and then back off the level so that the system is just ringing when somebody speaks into a mic. You can identify the frequency of this ring by pulling down the faders one at a time. If nothing happens, return the fader to its zero position and repeat the process with the next one – you'll eventually find one that makes the ringing stop. Pull this fader down by about 3dB and then turn up the system gain slowly until ringing starts again. If this ringing is at the same frequency, apply another 3dB of cut and continue with the process, or identify the new ring frequency and pull that back by 3dB. Repeat the process until all of the worst rings have been killed. Eventually you'll reach a point of diminishing returns where no further adjustments help, or where you've moved the faders so far that the quality of the sound is starting to suffer. Finally, to restore stability, pull the overall PA level down by at least 6dB from the point at which ringing occurs.

Ringing out applies both to the main PA and to the monitor system. If you're lucky, when the audience come in the feedback threshold will rise by as much as 5dB, as the sound is absorbed rather than reflected.

Main PA EQ

In all but the smallest systems it's common to use a graphic EQ in the main PA as well as in the monitor system, not only to tame feedback but also to obtain the best possible sound. Again, each venue has different sonic characteristics, so each will need a different EQ setting to make it sound good. Corrections should be carried out with EQ cut rather than boost, and the changes should be as subtle as possible. The reason for using only cut is that the human hearing system is far less sensitive to missing frequencies than it is to additional ones; a few decibels of cut applied at one frequency may be quite unnoticeable, but the same amount of boost applied at that frequency will be very obvious.

Some powered mixers come with five- or seven-band graphic equalisers built in, but although these are useful for general tone shaping or for countering the worst anomalies of a room they are too imprecise for controlling feedback or precision room compensation. Ideally, a stereo 30-band third-octave equaliser should be used.

Gigging

When you turn up at a venue, try to judge the best place to set up your gear before people start to assemble their kit. Find out where to position the main PA speakers – place them as far in front of you as is practical – and arrange them in such a way to produce the least problems with reflected sound. If the room is empty when you perform the soundcheck it may sound boomy, and feedback may occur at a lower level than you might like, but in most cases the situation improves when the audience arrives.

It's very important to direct as much sound into the audience as possible by positioning the speakers as recommended earlier. If possible, angle the speakers slightly downwards so that they are aimed at an imaginary point around two thirds towards the back of the room. By following the method described earlier you will be able to you tilt the cabinets without them becoming mechanically unstable – angling a tripod speaker by putting boxes beneath its legs is inviting an accident.

Backline Position

Try to set up the backline so that it's not directly behind the vocalists, and try to position the drums far enough back on the stage so that no one has a cymbal ringing in their ear. If you're a guitar player using a small combo it's a good idea to use a small stand to elevate it from the floor, but if you're also a singer you'll have to avoid setting it so high that it spills into your vocal mic. You could also move your guitar amp a little to one side so that you don't mask all of the sound with your body. If you stand in front of your amp, the sound heard by the audience will be duller than it should be. Also, if you decide to mic any of the back line, you should make sure that all of the mics are in place and that each one is working before soundchecking.

Setting The Mixer

It's important to position the mixer where you hear a representative sound from the speakers, but in small venues it's impractical to set up in the middle of the room with multicore trailing along the floor for people to fall over. More often than not you'll end up on one side, but you should avoid spots under balconies or in corners if at all possible because if you set up in these positions you'll hear more bass than is actually present in the rest of the room. Even if you're mixing near a side wall you'll hear a lift in the perceived sound of the bass, because of the boundary effect.

When you turn on the system, make sure that the mixer outputs are turned down, and switch the power amps on last of all or you might be greeted by a wall of feedback! Playing a song from your own CD collection through the system is a good way to get a feel for the acoustics of the venue. Next, ring out the system as best you can with the equalisers you have available and then drop the level to restore stability and leave you with a little headroom.

You should also check that each monitor speaker is working properly. Try working with the channel faders at around three quarters of the way up so that you still have some more level if you need it, and stick a piece of masking tape across the bottom of the console so that you can make a note of identifications for each channel.

The best way to tame an unruly system is to work at realistic sound levels; most audiences tend to think that bands are too loud anyway, so quality will always be appreciated more than quantity. The first thing you should do when soundchecking is establish a safe maximum working vocal level and then balance everything else to this. If the guitar amps are always too loud, consider using smaller combos or power soaks at smaller gigs so that they can be used at a lower level without sacrificing tone. It also helps to turn backing vocal mics either down or off completely when not using them because system gain – and hence the likelihood of feedback – is affected by the number of live mics which are open at any one time.

The drum kit will probably need some EQ applied to it before it sounds good. The settings shouldn't change that much from gig to gig, so perfect your default setting and then fine tune it so that you don't have to work from scratch every time. However, you should occasionally use the EQ bypass button just to make sure that the EQ'd sound is better than the original sound! Each drum, vocal and instrumental mic will need to be checked individually before you balance everything by running through a song. During this run-through you can fine tune the overall mix EQ with your graphic to make the best of the room's acoustics, and the sound will probably also dry up a little when the audience comes in.

If you're also accommodating a supporting act, it's important to make a precise note of your channel level, EQ and effects send settings before changing anything, as is keeping track of the movement of any mics.

Mixing Tips

Most genres of music demand that the vocals are heard, so always make sure that these are clearly audible and clear. If not, balance things by pulling down the backline level. After the vocal sound you'll need to get a good balance for the rhythm section, as this is the glue which holds the sound together. The drums and bass need to sit comfortably with each other, and if the drum sound is too boomy you may need to add a touch of low mid EQ cut to clean it up. Take notes on where solos appear in which songs and who plays them because you'll probably need to push their levels up by a couple of decibels to lift them above the rest of the band.

Perhaps the most important skill in live sound mixing is the ability to keep your eye on the ball all the time. You shouldn't find yourself constantly moving faders but you'll probably need to push levels up by a few decibels or so for solos, you'll need to cut mics that aren't being used, and you'll need to change effects patches as required. You must also make sure that you kill any vocal reverb between songs to keep the announcements clear, and don't push it back up until the next song starts – performers have a habit of announcing a song and then coming back to say something else, and it sounds terrible if the reverb is back up.

Acoustic Music

Mixing acoustic music is no more difficult than working with electric instruments, though you must be very certain that you're working well below the feedback level because of the number of mics you may be using. Sound will often leak from one mic to another, but this can sometimes be helpful because, if a mic is accidentally turned down when it's needed, the chances are that the performer will still be audible via the other mics, thus providing you with enough time to reset the correct level. As long as you make level changes slowly nobody will realise that you made a mistake!

Pay particular attention to the positions of the microphones, as the closer the performers are to their mics the fewer feedback problems you will experience and the better the overall separation will be.

The Self-Op PA

If you're operating you own mix from on stage, balance it while someone listens out front and then make as few changes as possible during the performance. Set up the mixer within arm's reach so that you can address any feedback problems simply by pulling down the master faders a touch. If there are any friends of the band who regularly come to your gigs and have a good ear for balance, ask them to report back on the sound during the show so that you can make changes where necessary. All that's needed is a few simple hand signals to indicate who's too loud and who's too quiet.

Another useful tip I've learned (the hard way!) is that, if you use an effects footswitch to turn the vocal reverb on and off, try to get one with an LED which indicates when it's activated, as it's difficult in some venues to tell whether the reverb is on or off.

Problems With Monitors

Musicians often complain that the monitors aren't loud enough, and this is a particular problem if somebody in the band has a quiet voice. Check the relative positions of the monitors and the mics anyway, and see if there are any drapes or curtains that can be used to mask off the back and side of the stage area to reduce sound reflections. If this problem occurs every time you play, you should seriously consider buying an automatic feedback suppressor. It could also help to supply the quiet singer with an in-ear monitor system.

Backing Tracks

A very large number of artists, ranging from top festival acts to solo club performers, depend on the use of backing tapes or other pre-recorded backing material. Many people still use cassette tapes because they're cheap, easy to copy, and the machines needed to play them are also cheap. Furthermore, commercially-available backing tapes are often available only on cassette, although as the public's awareness of sound quality continues to increase, side-effects such as hiss, wow and flutter, tonal dullness and pitch errors are no longer acceptable. There are now technically superior alternatives to cassettes, each with its own strengths and weaknesses.

DAT

DAT (Digital Audio Tape) machines offer the same sound quality as CDs and have incredibly fast winding speeds, allowing you to spin through a complete album in well under a minute, and there are also no problems with drifting pitches. Start IDs can be placed before each song so that you can cue up new songs quickly and precisely, and because DAT is a single-sided tape format you don't have the problems associated with turning the tape over.

DCC

Philips' DCC (Digital Compact Cassette) system is a consumer digital tape format that failed to take off, and so there are few machines around. However, they offer most of the advantages of DAT, although the fast wind time is slower. Check the availability of tapes before buying a DCC recorder.

Recordable Compact Disc

Transferring material onto CD-R (compact discs onto which you can record material only once) is inexpensive and guarantees high-quality sound and instant access to individual tracks. However, like vinyl, CD-Rs can jump if knocked or subjected to excessive vibration, and occasionally a dirty or scratched disc will jump with no provocation. At the very least you should sit your CD player on a thick slab of foam rubber. Treat the discs very carefully and always handle them by their edges.

MiniDisc

Sony's MiniDisc is yet another consumer recording format, and like DCC it uses data compression to cram more data onto the disc than would otherwise fit. The subjective sound quality is very similar to that of regular CDs, although not quite as good when heard over a high-quality hi-fi system. As the name suggests, MiniDisc machines use recordable discs rather than cassettes, which are built into a cartridge rather like a computer disk, but unlike CD-Rs – onto which material can only be recorded once – it's possible to record onto MiniDiscs multiple times, in much the same way as cassette.

The main benefits of the MiniDisc system are the same

as they are for CD-Rs, with the added bonus that you can record your own discs if your repertoire changes. MiniDisc recorders are cheaper than DAT machines and incorporate a powerful buffering system, which minimises the risk of the disc jumping due to vibration.

MIDI Files

While many performers buy pre-recorded backing tapes, there's a strong case for using commercially-available MIDI files to either create your own tapes or to create a 'live' synthesised backing supplied by a General MIDI sound module. The advantage of using MIDI files is that they contain only data; because they don't produce any sound on their own, the resulting sound can be changed depending on which synthesiser module or computer soundcard you use to play back the file. Perhaps more importantly, you can also customise the performance by changing the tempo or the key of the song, both of which may be adjusted independently, unlike on tape recordings, where playing back a cassette at a faster tempo also causes the pitch to increase.

Unless you have your own MIDI sequencer and synth, or a PC with suitable soundcard and software, you'll need to buy your MIDI files and then take them to a MIDI studio, which will turn them into backing tracks.

Live MIDI Backings

An alternative to using backing tapes on stage is to use a MIDI file player and a synth, and your safest bet is to use a hardware-based (as opposed to computer-based) system, as computers aren't suited to a life of travel. There are systems available which combine synthesiser and MIDI file player in the same box, and these are very attractive for the performer who needs to travel light.

8 THE TECHNICAL STUFF

Standard Levels

Most audio equipment used in live sound situations and in the studio is specified as working at either 'plus four' or 'minus ten', but what does that mean in practice? Plus four means that the equipment works at +4dBu, which is an operating level adopted in pro audio due to historic rather than logical reasons, and which corresponds to an RMS signal level of 1.23 volts. This is a fairly convenient operating level for use with modern op-amp circuitry as the circuitry is provided with a sensible amount of headroom before it runs into clipping problems.

The 'minus ten' level was introduced along with semi-professional recording equipment, and is largely a Japanese concept. Correctly stated, this value is -10dBV, which corresponds to 0.316 volts – roughly a third of a volt. Again, this is a reasonable level at which to use op-amp circuitry, but many purists feel that the +4dBu system provides a better balance between noise and headroom.

Resistance And Impedance

Loudspeakers, amplifiers, microphones, mixing consoles and even cables exhibit electrical resistance and impedance, and this becomes important when you start to connect different pieces together. If the impedance match isn't correct you could end up with signal loss, distortion, noise, or you could even damage something.

The term 'electrical resistance' is a means of describing a circuit's opposition to the DC current flowing through it – the higher the resistance of a circuit the higher the level of voltage needed to push current through it. Copper cable has a low electrical resistance and current flows through it easily, whereas plastic has a much higher electrical resistance and it's very difficult for current to flow through it. Materials with very high resistances, such as rubber, are known as insulators.

Ohm's Law

Resistance is measured in ohms, and there is a simple formula, known as Ohm's law, which establishes the relationship between current, voltage and resistance. If any two of these parameters are known, the third can easily be calculated by using the formula $R = V/I$, where V is the voltage across the circuit and I is the current (in amps) flowing through the circuit.

Because electrical power is defined as current multiplied by voltage, a subset of equally simple equations can be derived which relate power to current, voltage and resistance, the most useful of which are probably these: Power = V^2/R watts; and Power = I^2 x R watts.

Impedance

Knowing how to calculate resistance in a DC circuit is fine in theory, but in audio situations we're dealing with alternating currents right up to 20kHz or beyond – the upper threshold of human hearing. At these frequencies, circuitry ceases to behave as a pure resistor and instead exhibits impedance. However, viewing impedance as being AC resistance isn't too far from reality.

Impedance is still measured in ohms, and in a purely resistive circuit resistance and impedance are the same thing. In a circuit that has electrical capacitance and inductance as well as resistance, however, things starts to become more complicated. For example, a circuit which presents a capacitive load will experience a fall in impedance as the frequency rises, which is why capacitors are used in the filter circuits of devices such as equalisers and crossovers.

With audio equipment, it's desirable to keep the impedance reasonably constant over the entire audio range, although this isn't always possible. For example, loudspeaker impedance varies with frequency, and when the speaker is set in a cabinet the acoustic loading affects electrical impedance.

Input Impedance

Input impedance is related to the amount of current which the input terminals of a device draw from the device feeding it – the lower the impedance the more current required. If a circuit needs more current than can be provided by the circuit feeding it, there is a resulting mismatch.

Output impedance is a measure of the amount of current which an output can supply – the lower the output impedance the more current the unit can supply. It therefore stands to reason that, to pass a signal from one piece of equipment to another efficiently, the output impedance of the source must be either equal to or lower than the input impedance of the source. A factor of around five or ten times lower is not uncommon, although power amplifiers are an exception to this, and they have incredibly low output impedances.

The microphone input stage of typical mixing console has an impedance of around 1kohm, while a typical low-impedance dynamic mic has an impedance of between 15oohms and 20oohms or thereabouts, and this obviously provides a good match. Similarly, most pro audio line-level equipment has an input impedance of several tens of kohms (47kohms is a common figure), whereas output impedances are usually set as low as possible so that long cables can be driven without significant loss. Budget equipment, such as effects units, will typically have an output impedance of 1okohms or less, while professional equipment may have an output impedance of only a few tens of ohms.

Impedance Checklist

When connecting mic or line-level audio equipment, the source impedance should be significantly lower than the load impedance, ideally by a factor of five or more. If the load impedance is lower than the source impedance, the signal level will drop and there may also be audible distortion.

Note: never run valve amplifiers without a speaker connected to them as you may end up damaging them. Solid-state amps, however, usually survive this treatment.

When using cables in excess of ten metres, use low impedance sources to avoid signal degradation caused by cable impedance and external interference. Balanced systems offer greater immunity to interference than unbalanced systems, and on-stage line drivers with very long cable runs may be required.

With very high sources of impedance, such as electric guitars, cable length should be kept as short as is practical and a cable designed for guitar use should be used.

Loudspeaker Wiring

Speakers may be wired in series or parallel, as shown in Figure 8.1, and in such situations only speakers of the same impedance should be used together. The formula for resistance or impedance where devices are daisy-chained in series is this: $R = R_1 + R_2 + R_3$ and so on.

Parallel connections take a little more working out, involving the following formula: $\frac{1}{R} = \frac{1}{R_1} + \frac{1}{R_2} + \frac{1}{R_3}$. However, if the speakers all have the same impedance, as should be the case, the impedance of any number of parallel speakers is simply the impedance of one of the speakers divided by the total number of speakers. For example, two 8ohm speakers in parallel produce a total load of eight divided by two, or 4ohms.

Gain Structure

It is the nature of sound that it covers a vast dynamic range, from the dropping of a pin to the exploding of

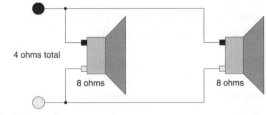

4 ohms total

8 ohms

8 ohms

Parallel connection

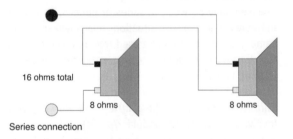

16 ohms total

8 ohms

8 ohms

Series connection

a tank shell, and reproducing this range with an equivalent analogue electronic signal results in a signal level that might vary from less than a microvolt (a millionth of a volt) up to ten volts or so. In a typical PA mixer, the signal from a microphone is amplified to bring it up to line level, which is the nominal operating level of the system (+4dBu, for example). The signal is then passed through a whole chain of circuitry, where it is equalised, routed, mixed and effected before being passed on to the power amplifiers.

The problem involved with processing analogue signals is that each and every piece of circuitry adds noise to the signal – there's no such thing as noise-free circuitry. This noise is actually caused by the random movement of electrons, and until we find some way around the limitations set by quantum mechanics we're stuck with it. Fortunately, a well-designed circuit adds only a tiny amount of noise, and this is largely constant. It's therefore pretty obvious that, if you feed a very low-level signal through the circuit, the ratio of noise to wanted signal is going to be worse than if you feed a strong signal through the circuit. However, there is a limit to how hot your signal can be; if it's too high in level it will cause the circuitry to clip, and you'll hear distortion.

Optimum Levels

The secret is to find a compromise where the signal level is kept reasonably high but there is still a little safety margin, or headroom, to accommodate any unexpected signal peaks. This concept makes more sense if you can visualise the VU meters on a mixing console. The nominal operating level is the level at which the signal peaks at around the oVU mark (where the red area starts), and the amount of headroom is determined as being the distance which you can push the level into the red before you hear distortion.

Most analogue circuits don't suddenly clip when the level gets too high; instead, the amount of distortion rises gradually as the last few decibels of headroom are used up, after which hard clipping occurs.

Digital Level Settings

Digital circuits have similar limitations to their analogue counterparts – if the signal is too high in level it will still clip when the maximum numerical value which the system can handle is exceeded. However, there isn't the same safety margin or area of progressive distortion as there is with analogue circuitry – the signal may be perfect, but push it up another decibel or so and you hear clipping. For this reason the nominal operating level for digital equipment is usually chosen to be around 12dB or so below the actual oVU mark, or clipping point, in order to leave a useful amount of headroom. This is important when setting up a send level to digital effects.

If too small a signal is fed into a digital system it is represented by fewer bits, which means that the signal suffers from quantising distortion, and this sounds very much like noise. In other words, using digital circuitry doesn't mean that you don't have to worry about noise – you still have too feed it a signal at the right level.

Optimising Gain Structure

Perhaps the most important place to get the gain structure right is at the start of the audio chain, especially if you're using microphones. Always use the channel PFL buttons on your mixer to help you set individual input gain trim controls so that the peak signal is just edging into the red on the console's PFL meters. It takes a few minutes to set all of your mics individually, but it's something that must be done religiously if the best signal is to be achieved. If you always use the same mics in the same channels, and if the PA is used only by your band, you could make a note of the input gain trim settings so that you don't have to set them at every gig.

Send Levels

Another potential source of trouble is the external effects unit. If your console effects send controls are turned to a low setting, and if you then turn up the input stage of your effects unit to compensate, you'll end up with more noise than you would if you had the console levels set higher and the effects input level set lower. The best scenario for line-level signals is to maintain a unity gain situation wherever possible – in other words, the signal should stay at nominally the same level rather than constantly built up and then knocked down again, or vice versa. On most mixers a send setting of around seven corresponds to unity gain, and the same is true of the master send control. If you make sure that the channel with the highest send setting is set to around seven, you won't go too far wrong.

If your effects unit has an output level control, this should also be set at around seven, or to the unity gain position, which means that the actual level of effect is determined by the effects return control on your desk.

Cables And Connections

One of the less glamorous aspects of live sound is the amount of cabling required to have a system up and running. In a typical audio system all of the signal cables should be screened, other than those linking the power amplifiers to the speakers. The purpose of the screen is to intercept electrostatic interference and drain it away to earth before it can affect the signals passing along the inner wires. In an unbalanced cable the screen also forms the signal return conductor, whereas in a balanced cable the signal is carried by the two cores and the screen does not constitute a part of the audio signal path.

The screen may comprise a woven copper braid, layers of multistrand wire wrapped around the inner cores in a spiral fashion, a thin layer of metal foil, or even conductive plastic. Each type of cable has its own strengths and weaknesses, in terms of screening efficiency, flexibility, cable capacitance, ease of termination and so on.

Multicores

The type of multicore cable used to feed mic signals from the stage to the mixer comprises a number of small-diameter, individually-screened, twin-core cables housed in a common outer sleeve. Multicores are used in fixed installations and for connecting the mixing console to the stage box in conventional PA applications.

Speaker Cables

The function of a speaker cable is to provide a path of low resistance between the amplifier and the loudspeaker, and if the cable resistance compared to the impedance of the speakers to which it is connected is significant, the power will be shared between the speaker and the cable.

Using inadequate cable will also reduce the damping factor of the amplifier, where the damping factor is defined as the output impedance of the amplifier divided into the impedance of the speaker to which it is connected. This is an important point, because the higher the damping factor the greater the amplifier's ability to produce a tight, accurate bass end. The damping factor becomes less effective as the cable impedance rises.

Use the shortest, thickest speaker leads you can, make sure speaker cables are roughly the same length, and use low-resistance connectors such as Speakons or XLRs. Jack connectors are a poor compromise, even on low-powered systems.

Balanced Wiring

Signal connections on an analogue audio system may be either balanced or unbalanced. An unbalanced connection relies on a two-conductor cable, and in a screened audio cable this comprises a central core surrounded by a conductive screen. Although the screen (which is generally connected to ground) offers a significant degree of protection against electromagnetic interference, it's still possible for traces of outside interference to be superimposed on the wanted signal.

Balanced systems were developed to provide increased immunity to electromagnetic interference, and the principle is very simple. Instead of a two-conductor system, balancing is achieved by using three conductors – one of these is still an outer screen, while the other two are inner wires which carry the signal. Two signal cables are used here because one must be fed with a phase-inverted version of the signal, and if you look at the wiring details for a balanced connector (usually an XLR or stereo jack) you'll see that the normal signal connection is usually referred to as 'plus' or 'hot', while the inverted signal is 'minus' or 'cold'.

At the receiving equipment, the minus (inverted) signal is inverted once again to bring it back into phase with the plus (normal) signal, and the two are combined. Why does this help? Because the two signal wires are physically very close to each other, it's reasonable to assume that any interference will affect both conductors pretty much equally. When the minus signal is re-inverted at the receiving end, any interference on that line will also be inverted, so when the plus and minus signals are added the overall result is that the two interference signals cancel each other out, while the wanted signals combine. Figure 8.2 describes both balanced and unbalanced connection systems.

Ground Loops

Ground loops are a potential problem in any complex audio system where there are multiple earth paths

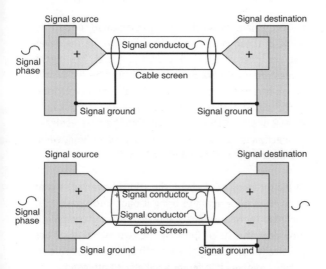

Note that, in a balanced system, the screen
may often be left disconnected at the source
end to help prevent ground loops

Figure 8.2: Balanced audio connections

between pieces of equipment and the mains supply
ground. Your effects, processors, mixers, power
amplifiers and back line may function perfectly in
isolation, but if you connect them together the chances
are that you'll hear at least some background hum. If
you're lucky this will be fairly quiet, but if you're unlucky

it may prove to be so intrusive that your system becomes unusable.

Disconnecting the earth cables from various mains plugs is not a very safe option, especially in live situations, where performers are in close proximity with both grounded metalwork and mains-powered amplification.

Unbalanced Audio Systems

Simple audio systems rely largely on unbalanced audio connections, in which the signal travels along screened cables, each comprising a single insulated core surrounded by a screen, which is grounded to prevent outside electrical interference from reaching the signal. However, this isn't a foolproof arrangement.

All cable has an electrical resistance, and although this may be fairly low it is nonetheless discernible. If an electrical current is passed through any material that has an electrical resistance, a voltage will be produced between the two points of contact, and the magnitude of this will depend on the strength of the current and the resistance of the material, as stated by Ohm's law. It therefore follows that, if a current is passed through the screen of a cable, there will then be a difference in voltage between one end of the screen and the other, which can cause problems with ground loops.

The Ground Loop

All audio systems include numerous mains-powered pieces of equipment joined to each other via cables, and there may be problems if all or part of this system uses unbalanced connections. All of the signal screens and mains earths will interconnect, and because cable possesses resistance there's a real danger that interference signals will cause current to flow in the cable screens, resulting in audible signal contamination. While most interfering signals are pretty feeble, such as signals from distant radio transmitters, the 50/60Hz mains supply is a different matter. If you were to place a closed loop of wire inside a studio you'd be able to measure a 50/60Hz current flow in the wire, because the loop acts exactly like an inefficient transformer, picking up hum from wiring and transformers in other equipment. Even the most inefficient coupling of the mains supply into a wire loop will produce enough current to generate a voltage, which will be audible as hum.

While the loop of wire in this example is purely hypothetical, Figure 8.3 clearly illustrates how the earth and screen connections between just two pieces of equipment can form a closed loop, which will be affected by induced mains hum. In reality the wiring in a typical system is likely to create many ground loops, all of which will interact with each other. In Figure 8.3 the circuit is completed by the mains lead grounds and the signal cable screens to form a single-turn transformer.

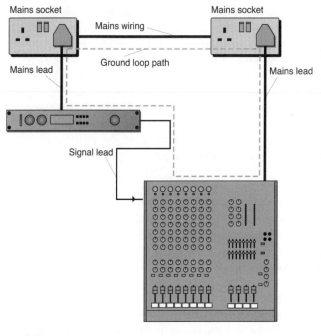

Figure 8.3: Anatomy of a ground loop

Breaking Loops

To reduce or eliminate the effects of ground loops, each piece of equipment should have only one ground current path between it and the rest of the system to which it is connected. To comply with this rule, it's necessary to locate any ground loops and break them in some way, and this creates a dilemma: either the signal screen must be disconnected at some point to break the loop or the mains earth must be removed and the signal screens must stay connected.

While the latter approach may work, removing the mains ground connection is potentially dangerous and quite possibly illegal. What's more, if the signal lead is unplugged, the earth protection is completely removed.

Note that equipment operating from external mains two-pin mains adaptors is designed to be used unearthed, and so may be less susceptible to ground-loop problems, as is often the case with effects units powered by adaptor plugs. However, if the unit is bolted to a metal rack, a loop may be created via the casework of the unit.

Remedies

In professional studios, where everything is balanced, disconnecting the screen at one end of a signal cable will usually cure any hum problems because the screen isn't used as a return path for the signal – it's purely a protective screen. In an unbalanced system, however, disconnecting one end of a screen can cause difficulties because you will then be relying on the mains cable earth to act as return path for the audio signal. This can lead to RF interference problems, and if the mains cable is then removed this will leave you with no return path at all, and you'll be greeted by a very loud hum!

A simple remedy is to connect a small resistor in series with the screen at one end of the cable, as shown in Figure 8.4. In a typical audio system a resistor of around 100ohms will be high enough to significantly reduce any induced hum currents while still being low enough for it not to affect the level of the signal passing through the cable. If you still experience high-frequency whistles, or breakthrough from radio stations, a 1nf (nanofarad) capacitor, connected in parallel with the resistor, should help. A quarter- (or even eighth-) watt metal oxide film resistor can be mounted inside most plastic-bodied jack plugs without difficulty. Figure 8.4 also shows how the capacitor is wired, should you decide to add one.

This method of tackling ground loops is a compromise, but it can still bring about a dramatic reduction in the level of hum in a system which uses unbalanced cables.

This is how the resistor is wired
between the screen of the cable
and the earth tag of the jack plug

This is how the resistor will
look when the cable has been
clamped into the plug

This end of the lead is
wired conventionally

100 picofarads

A capacitor is fitted across the
resistor to reduce susceptibility to RF
interference

Figure 8.4: Making a ground lift lead

Unbalanced To Balanced

If you have a desk with balanced line inputs but your
outboard gear is unbalanced, you can improve things
still further, as shown in Figure 8.5. This approach is
more satisfactory than the practise of putting a resistor
in series with the screen in a completely unbalanced
circuit because you're not relying on the screen to act
as a return path for the signal – it works purely as a
protective screen against interference.

Ground Compensation

Some mixing consoles use a fake balancing system known as ground compensation. Details of how to connect both balanced and unbalanced signals to these mixers should be included in the console's handbook, and in most instances the additional effort involved in making or adapting cables to take advantage of these inputs is very worthwhile.

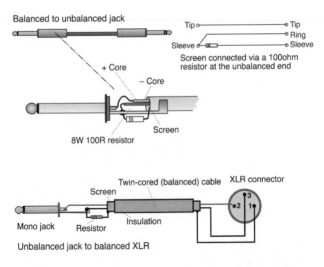

Figure 8.5: Unbalanced to balanced connection

When laying out your cables you should try not to run signal cables alongside mains cable for any distance, as this can also produce hum. You should also be aware that anything containing a large transformer is liable to radiate a strong hum field, so power amps and mixer power supplies should be mounted away from other processors. At the very least, leave a few U of empty rack space between these items and your effects processors.

Ground Lift

If you draw a wiring diagram for your system, including all of the signal cables and mains leads (only those with earths, not mains adaptors), you'll soon see where the potential ground-loop problems lie. However, problems also arise when a ground signal path is completed by another route, for example the metalwork of a rack system. Some rack equipment is fitted with an internal ground lift, which can be either fixed or switchable in its operation, and which reduces the risk of encountering ground loops when unbalanced connecting cables are used. Conversely, balanced equipment should always have the metalwork grounded.

Ground-Loop Checklist

- Don't disconnect the earth leads from pieces of equipment that are designed to be used grounded.

- Build up your system a piece at a time, checking for hum at every stage. Cure any ground-loop problems before connecting any more equipment. If you don't experience any hum problems when using standard leads, don't feel that you have to fit ground-lifted cables (see Figure 8.4) – move onto the next piece of equipment.

- Use balanced wiring where practical.

- Use ground-lifted leads when working with unbalanced equipment to ensure that each piece of equipment has only one direct earth path, either via a mains earth or a signal cable screen. Use a modified balanced cable when connecting unbalanced sources to balanced destinations, as shown in Figure 8.5.

  With two-pin mains equipment, or equipment running from mains adaptors, treat each device as you would for ground-lifted equipment, and ensure that just one of the signal cables provides a true ground. Additional connections should also be ground lifted (via resistors, in the case of unbalanced units) if further problems arise. If you don't find a problem don't feel that you have to provide a cure.

- Check individual items of equipment with a meter to determine which devices are equipped with built-in ground-lift resistors. Those that are ground lifted should be grounded via both the mains and one signal cable.

- Beware of problems caused by case-to-case contact. This is common in metal racks and is usually cured by using nylon mounting hardware.

- Make sure that all of your special cables are clearly marked, such as those which are equipped with resistors.

Soldering

Running even a small PA system involves a certain amount of maintenance, most involving checking and repairing your cables. If you're putting together a new system you may also find that you have to make some of the cables yourself, in those cases where suitable off-the-shelf cables are unavailable. At the heart of cable maintenance is the practice of soldering.

You'll need a soldering iron of around 30-50 watts with a plated bit (the soldering tip) – plated tips last much longer than copper varieties and can be cleaned during use by simply wiping away excess or oxidised solder with a piece of cotton rag or a special moistened sponge – not foam rubber! As well as the iron you'll also need some wire cutters, a pair of small electrical pliers (the type that taper to a point), a pair of wire strippers and a reel of multicore solder. These can join the rest of your travelling tool kit, which should at the very least include a torch, a multimeter, some spare fuses and connectors, assorted screwdrivers, an adjustable spanner and a reel of insulation tape, not to mention gaffa tape (duct tape in America).

Multicore solder is made with several cores of chemical flux sealed inside the solder itself. This flux is vital in keeping the joint free of oxide while it is being made. You may also find that you need a miniature vice, but when soldering jacks or XLRs I usually plug them into my cable tester to hold them still while I solder them.

Tinning

If a connector has holes to allow a wire to pass through (as jack plugs often have), the easiest way to work is to first strip the end of the wire and then tin it, using the soldering iron. Tinning is the process of applying solder to each of the two parts to be joined prior to final assembly. Bring the soldering iron, the wire end and the solder together and you should see the solder melt and flow onto the wire end. The individual strands of wire should soak up the solder like a sponge so that you're left with a single solder-coated strand. Never try to carry solder to the job on the end of the iron – all that will happen is that the flux will boil off and then, when you try to get the solder to flow onto the wire, it will produce a pasty blob. It's vital that the solder is melted at the location of the joint so that, as soon as the flux in the solder is heated, it can flow onto the wire. You'll find that you'll need to wipe the iron fairly frequently to keep the tip clean.

Most connectors are either pre-tinned or have a surface plating that doesn't need tinning, in which case the tinned wire ends can be pushed through the holes in the connector terminals and then bent over with pliers so that they don't fall out when the joint is completed. When the connector is held firmly in a vice or spare socket, apply just a little solder to the tip of the iron to wet it, bring the iron to the joint to heat it up for a few seconds, and then feed in a little solder between the tip of the iron and the joint. If the joint is hot enough, the solder will flow smoothly and fill any gaps between the wire and the terminal. As soon as this happens, remove the heat and keep the joint very still for ten seconds or more until the solder has solidified. If the joint is moved while the solder is setting this may cause the solder to crystallise, producing a dry joint. If the joint isn't hot enough, or if you've tried to carry solder on the tip of the iron, the solder won't flow and you'll end up with either no joint at all or a dry joint. A dry joint is one on which you've managed to get some solder to stick but there isn't enough of a connection between the two parts to make electrical contact. A good joint should be shiny, and the solder should have flowed smoothly along the terminal, away from the joint in all directions, as shown in Figure 8.6.

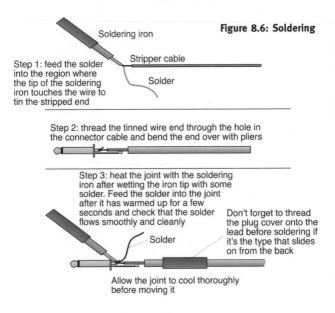

Figure 8.6: Soldering

Soldering iron

Stripper cable

Solder

Step 1: feed the solder into the region where the tip of the soldering iron touches the wire to tin the stripped end

Step 2: thread the tinned wire end through the hole in the connector cable and bend the end over with pliers

Step 3: heat the joint with the soldering iron after wetting the iron tip with some solder. Feed the solder into the joint after it has warmed up for a few seconds and check that the solder flows smoothly and cleanly

Solder

Don't forget to thread the plug cover onto the lead before soldering if it's the type that slides on from the back

Allow the joint to cool thoroughly before moving it

Figure 8.6: Soldering (continued)

Note that the solder has
flowed smoothly around
and through the joint

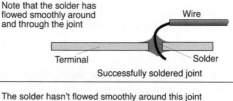

Wire

Terminal

Solder

Successfully soldered joint

The solder hasn't flowed smoothly around this joint
but instead has formed into blobs. This is a sign
that either joint was not hot enough or that all the
flux had been boiled away before the joint could
be made. If this happens, simply apply fresh
solder and start again

Terminal

Solder

Badly soldered joint

APPENDIX
Common Cable Connections

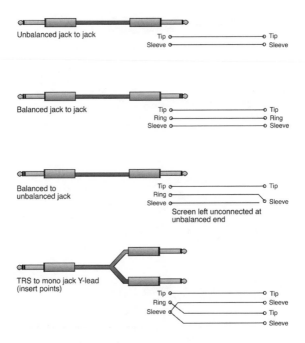

Unbalanced jack to jack

Tip o————————o Tip
Sleeve o————————o Sleeve

Balanced jack to jack

Tip o————————o Tip
Ring o————————o Ring
Sleeve o————————o Sleeve

Balanced to
unbalanced jack

Tip o————————o Tip
Ring o————
Sleeve o————————o Sleeve

Screen left unconnected at
unbalanced end

TRS to mono jack Y-lead
(insert points)

Tip o————————o Tip
Ring o————————o Sleeve
Sleeve o————————o Tip
————————o Sleeve

basic Live Sound

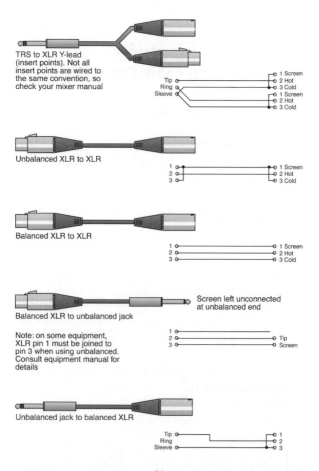

TRS to XLR Y-lead
(insert points). Not all
insert points are wired to
the same convention, so
check your mixer manual

Tip
Ring
Sleeve

1 Screen
2 Hot
3 Cold
1 Screen
2 Hot
3 Cold

Unbalanced XLR to XLR

1
2
3

1 Screen
2 Hot
3 Cold

Balanced XLR to XLR

1
2
3

1 Screen
2 Hot
3 Cold

Balanced XLR to unbalanced jack

Screen left unconnected
at unbalanced end

Note: on some equipment,
XLR pin 1 must be joined to
pin 3 when using unbalanced.
Consult equipment manual for
details

1
2
3

Tip
Screen

Unbalanced jack to balanced XLR

Tip
Ring
Sleeve

1
2
3

GLOSSARY

Acoustic Feedback

Loud audible howling sound caused by the sound from a loudspeaker being picked up by a microphone and re-amplified.

Active

Circuit using electrical power to amplify or process signals.

AFL

After-Fade Listen. Used in mixing desks to allow specific signals to be monitored at the level set by their fader or level control knob. Aux sends are generally monitored AFL rather than PFL so that the signal being fed to an effects unit can be monitored.

Algorithm

Computer program designed to perform a specific task. In the context of effects units, algorithms usually describe a software building block designed to create a specific effect or combination of effects. All digital effects are based on algorithms.

Analogue
Circuitry that uses a continually-changing voltage or current to represent a signal. The origin of the term is that the electrical signal can be thought of as being analogous to the original signal.

Attack
Time taken for a sound to achieve maximum amplitude. Drums have a fast attack, whereas bowed strings have a slow attack. In compressors and gates, the attack time equates to how quickly the processor can change its gain.

Attenuate
To make lower in level.

Audio Frequency
That part of the sound spectrum audible to humans, generally held to range from around 20Hz-20kHz.

Aux
Control on a mixer designed to route a proportion of the channel signal to the effects or cue mix outputs (see *Aux Send*).

Aux Return
Mixer inputs used to add effects to the mix.

Aux Send

Physical output from a mixer aux send buss.

Backline

On-stage instrument amplification.

Balance

Relative levels of the left and right channels of a stereo recording. Also describes the relative levels of instruments and voices within a mix.

Balanced Wiring

Wiring system which uses two out-of-phase conductors and a common screen to reduce the effect of interference. For balancing to be effective, both the sending and receiving device must have balanced output and input stages respectively.

Bandwidth

Means of specifying the range of frequencies passed by an electronic circuit such as an amplifier, mixer or filter. The frequency range is usually measured at the points at which the level drops by 3dB relative to the maximum.

Bit

Binary digit, which may either be one or zero.

Boost/Cut Control

Single control which allows the range of frequencies passing through a filter to be either amplified or attenuated. The centre position is usually the 'flat' or 'no effect' position.

Buss

Common electrical signal path along which signals may travel. In a mixer, there are several busses carrying the stereo mix, the groups, the PFL signal, the aux sends and so on. Power supplies are also fed along busses.

Capacitor Microphone

Mic operating on the principle of changing electrical capacitance between a stationary electrode and a moving, electrically-conductive diaphragm. Capacitor mics require power to polarise the capacitive pickup element and to run the internal pre-amp.

Cardioid

Meaning heart shaped, describes the polar response of a unidirectional mic, which picks up sound over a narrow angle.

Channel

In the context of mixing consoles, a channel is a single strip of controls relating to one input.

Chorus
Effect created by doubling a signal and adding delay and pitch modulation.

Clipping
Severe form of distortion which occurs when a signal tries to exceed the highest level which a piece of equipment can handle.

Compander
Encode/decode device that compresses a signal while encoding it, then expands it when decoding it.

Compressor
Device which reduces the dynamic range of audio signals by reducing levels of high signals or boosting those of low signals.

Conductor
Material that provides low resistance for electrical current.

Crossover
Electrical or electronic circuit designed to route only high frequencies to the tweeters and low frequencies to the bass speakers, or 'woofers'.

Cutoff Frequency

Frequency above or below which attenuation begins in a filter circuit.

Cycle
One complete vibration of a sound source or its electrical equivalent. One cycle per second is expressed as one Hertz (Hz).

Daisy Chain
Term used to describe serial electrical connection between devices or modules.

Damping
In terms of reverb, refers to the rate at which reverberant energy is absorbed by the various surfaces in an environment.

DAT
Digital Audio Tape. The most commonly-used DAT machines are actually R-DATs, because they use a rotating head. Digital recorders using fixed heads (such as DCC) are known as S-DAT machines.

Data Compression
System for reducing the amount of data stored by a digital system. Most audio data compression systems are known as lossy systems, as some of the original

signal is discarded in accordance with psychoacoustic principles designed to ensure that only components which cannot be heard are lost.

dB

Decibel. Unit used to express the relative levels of two electrical voltages, powers or sounds.

dBv

Variation on dB referenced to odB = 0.775v.

dBV

Variation on dB referenced to odB = 1V.

DCC

Stationary-head digital recorder format developed by Philips. Uses a data-compression system to reduce the amount of data that needs to be stored.

DDL

Digital Delay Line.

DI

Direct Inject, in which a signal is plugged directly into an audio chain without using a mic. A DI box matches the signal-level impedance of a source to a tape machine or mixer input.

Digital
Electronic system which represents data and signals in the form of codes comprising ones and zeros.

Digital Delay
Digital processor for generating delay and echo effects.

Digital Reverb
Digital processor for simulating reverberation.

DIN Connector
Consumer multipin signal connection format, also used for MIDI cabling. Various pin configurations are available.

Directivity
Describes the angle of coverage of a loudspeaker system in both the vertical and horizontal planes. Higher directivity equates to a narrower angle of coverage.

Dry
Signal to which no effects have been added. Wet sounds are those which have been treated with an effect, such as reverberation.

Dynamic Microphone
Mic that works on the electric generator principle,

whereby a diaphragm moves a coil of wire within a magnetic field.

Dynamic Range
Range measured in decibels between the highest signal that can be handled by a piece of equipment and the level at which small signals disappear into the noise floor.

Dynamics
Way of describing the relative levels within a piece of music.

Early Reflections
First sound reflections from walls, floors and ceilings following a sound which is created in an acoustically reflective environment.

Effects Return
Additional mixer input designed to accommodate the output from an effects unit.

Effects Unit
Device for treating an audio signal in order to change it in some creative way. Effects often involve the use of delay circuits, and include such treatments as reverb and echo.

Enhancer
Device which brightens audio material using techniques like dynamic equalisation, phase shifting and harmonic generation.

Envelope
How the level of a sound or signal varies over time.

Equaliser
Device for cutting or boosting parts of the audio spectrum.

Exciter
Enhancer that synthesises new high-frequency harmonics.

Expander
Device designed to decrease the level of low-level signals and increase the level of high-level signals, thus increasing the dynamic range of the signal.

Fader
Sliding control used in mixers and other processors.

Figure-Of-Eight
Describes the polar response of a mic that is equally sensitive at both front and rear, yet rejects sounds coming from the sides.

Filter
Electronic circuit designed to emphasise or attenuate a specific range of frequencies.

Flanging
Modulated delay effect using feedback to create a dramatic, sweeping sound.

Foldback
System for feeding one or more separate mixes to the performers for use while recording and overdubbing. Also known as a cue mix.

Frequency
Indication of how many cycles of a repetitive waveform occur in the space of one second. A waveform which has a repetition cycle of once per second has a frequency of 1Hz.

Frequency Response
Measurement of the frequency range that can be handled by a specific piece of electrical equipment or loudspeaker.

Fundamental
Any sound comprises a fundamental or basic frequency plus harmonics and partials at a higher frequency.

Gain
Amount by which a circuit amplifies a signal.

Gate
Device designed to mute low-level signals, thus improving the noise performance during pauses in the wanted material.

Graphic Equaliser
Equaliser on which several narrow segments of the audio spectrum are controlled by individual cut/boost faders. The name derives from the fact that the fader positions provide a graphic representation of the EQ curve.

Ground
Electrical earth, or zero volts. In mains wiring, the ground cable is connected to the ground via a long conductive metal spike.

Ground Loops
Also known as earth loops. Wiring problem in which currents circulate in the ground wiring of an audio system, known as the ground loop effect. When these currents are induced by the alternating mains supply, hum results.

Group
Collection of signals within a mixer that are mixed and

routed through a separate fader to provide overall control. In multitrack mixers, several groups are provided to feed recorder track inputs.

Harmonic
High-frequency component of a complex waveform.

Head
Part of a tape machine or disk drive that reads and/or writes data to and from the storage media.

Headroom
The safety margin in decibels between the highest peak signal being passed by a piece of equipment and the absolute maximum level the equipment can handle.

High-Pass Filter
Filter which attenuates frequencies below its cutoff frequency.

Horn Tweeter
High-frequency loudspeaker which has a horn-shaped flare fixed to the front in order to increase the acoustic efficiency and better control the directivity.

Hz
Shorthand for Hertz, the unit of frequency.

Impedance

Can be visualised as the AC resistance of a circuit which contains both resistive and reactive components.

Inductor

Reactive component which presents an impedance with increases with frequency.

In-Ear Monitoring

Relatively recent innovation which uses miniature in-ear phones in place of on-stage monitor loudspeakers.

Insert Point

Connector that allows an external processor to be patched into a signal path so that the signal flows through the processor.

Jack

Commonly used mono (TS) or stereo (TRS) audio connector.

LED

Light-Emitting Diode, a solid-state lamp.

Limiter

Device that controls the gain of a signal so as to prevent it from ever exceeding a preset level. A limiter is essentially a fast-acting compressor with an infinite compression ratio.

Line Level

Standard signal level at which mixers and signal processors tend to work. In practice there are several different line levels, but all are in the order of a few volts. A nominal signal level is around 10dBv for semi-pro and +4dBv for professional equipment.

Low-Frequency Oscillator (LFO)

Oscillator used as a modulation source, usually below 20Hz. The most common waveshape is the sine wave, though there is often a choice of sine, square, triangular and sawtooth waveforms.

Low-Pass Filter

A filter which attenuates frequencies above its cutoff frequency.

MIDI

Musical Instrument Digital Interface.

(Standard) MIDI File

Standard file for storing MIDI sequencer song data in such a way that it can be read by other makes or models of MIDI sequencer.

Mixer/Amplifier

Single unit containing both mixer and power amplifier(s).

Monitor

Reference loudspeaker used for mixing, or the action of listening to a mix or a specific audio signal.

Monophonic

One note at a time.

Multicore Cable

Type of cable used to connect stage mics to a remote mixer. Comprises several individually-screened cable pairs within a single flexible outer sheath.

Noise Reduction

System for reducing analogue tape noise or for reducing the level of hiss present in a recording.

Omni

Refers to a microphone that is equally sensitive in all directions, or to the MIDI mode in which data on all channels is recognised.

Oscillator

Circuit designed to generate a periodic electrical waveform.

Pad

Resistive circuit for reducing signal level.

Pan Pot

Control enabling the user of a mixer to move the signal to any point in the stereo soundstage by varying the relative levels fed to the left and right stereo outputs.

Parallel

Method of connecting two or more circuits together so that their inputs and outputs are all connected together.

Parametric EQ

Equaliser with controls for frequency, bandwidth and cut/boost.

Passive

Describes a circuit with no active elements.

Passive Two-Way

Refers to a loudspeaker system comprising a bass driver and a tweeter fed from a passive crossover filter network, comprising capacitors, resistors and inductors.

PFL

Pre-Fade Listen. A system used within a mixing console to allow the operator to listen in on a selected signal, regardless of the position of the fader controlling that signal.

Phantom Power
48v DC supply for capacitor microphones, transmitted along the signal cores of a balanced mic cable.

Phase
Timing difference between two electrical waveforms expressed in degrees where 360º corresponds to a delay of one cycle.

Phaser
Effect combining a signal with a phase-shifted version of itself to produce filtering effects. Most are controlled by means of an LFO.

Pickup
Part of a guitar that converts string vibrations to electrical signals.

Pitch Shifter
Device for changing the pitch of an audio signal without changing its duration.

Post-Fade
Aux signal taken from after the channel fader so that

the aux send level follows any channel fader changes. Normally used for feeding effects devices.

Power Amplifier
Amplifier designed to accept line-level signals and boost them to the high power levels necessary to drive loudspeakers. Most professional models have two channels, for stereo operation.

Pre-Fade
Aux signal taken from before the channel fader so that the channel fader has no effect on the aux send level. The pre-fade is normally used for creating foldback or cue mixes.

Processor
Devices such as compressors, gates and equalisers, which treat audio signals by changing their dynamics or frequency contents.

Q
Measurement of the resonant properties of a filter. The higher the Q, the more resonant the filter and the narrower the range of frequencies that are allowed to pass.

Release
Time taken for a level or gain to return to normal. Often

used to describe the rate at which a synthesised sound reduces in level after a key has been released.

Resonance
Same as Q.

RMS
Root Mean Square. A method of specifying the behaviour of electrical equipment under continuous sine wave testing.

Roll-Off
Rate at which a filter attenuates a signal once it has passed the filter cutoff point.

Side Chain
Part of a circuit that splits off part of the main signal to be processed. Compressors derive their control signals from side-chain signals.

Speaker Column
Enclosure in which the loudspeakers are arranged in a vertical row.

Spill
Leaking of sound from speakers or other sources into live mics.

SPL
Sound-Pressure Level. Measured in decibels.

Stage Box
Box fitted with multiple connectors, usually XLRs, enabling microphones to be fed into a multicore.

Stage Monitoring
System of amps and loudspeakers which enables the performers on the stage to hear what they are playing and singing.

Stereo
Two-channel system feeding both left and right loudspeakers.

Sub-Bass
Frequencies below the range of monitor loudspeakers, defined by some as those that are felt rather than heard.

Sync
System for making two or more pieces of equipment run in synchronism with each other.

Synthesiser
Electronic musical instrument designed to create a wide range of sounds, both imitative and abstract.

Timbre

Tonal 'colour' of a sound.

Transducer

Device which converts one form of energy into another. A mic is a transducer, as it converts mechanical to electrical energy.

Tremolo

Modulation of the amplitude of a sound using an LFO.

Tweeter

Loudspeaker designed to reproduce high frequencies.

Unbalanced

Describes a two-wire electrical signal connection where the inner (or hot, or positive) conductor is usually surrounded by the outer (or cold, or negative) conductor, forming a screen against interference.

Vibrato

Pitch modulation using an LFO to modulate a VCO.

XLR

Type of connector commonly used to carry balanced audio signals, including the feeds from microphones.

6/11(178714)